Mandala
Fancy Coloring Books

Copyright: Published in the United States by Lora Frierson
Published January 2017
ISBN-13: 978-1542344395
ISBN-10: 1542344395

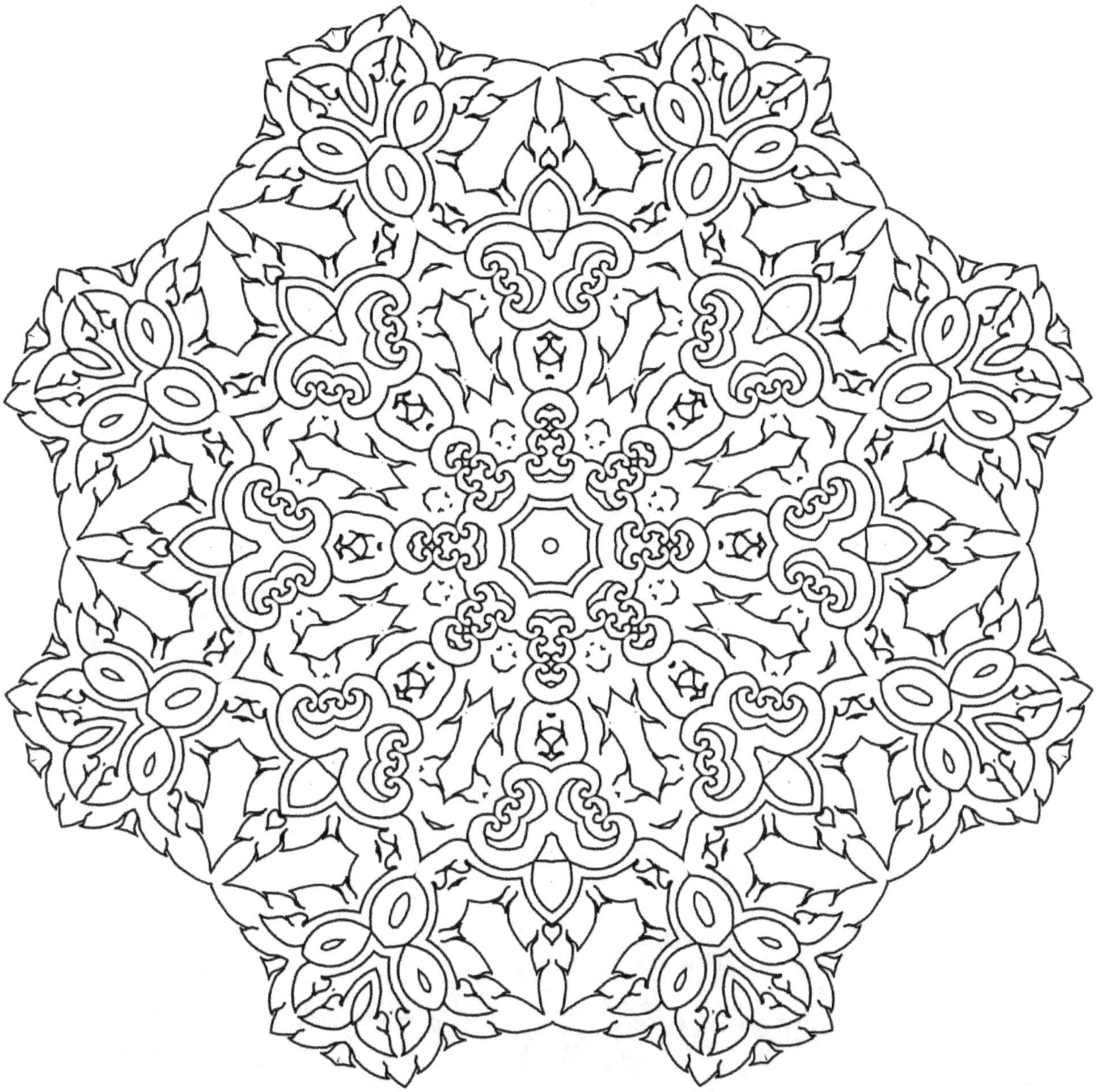

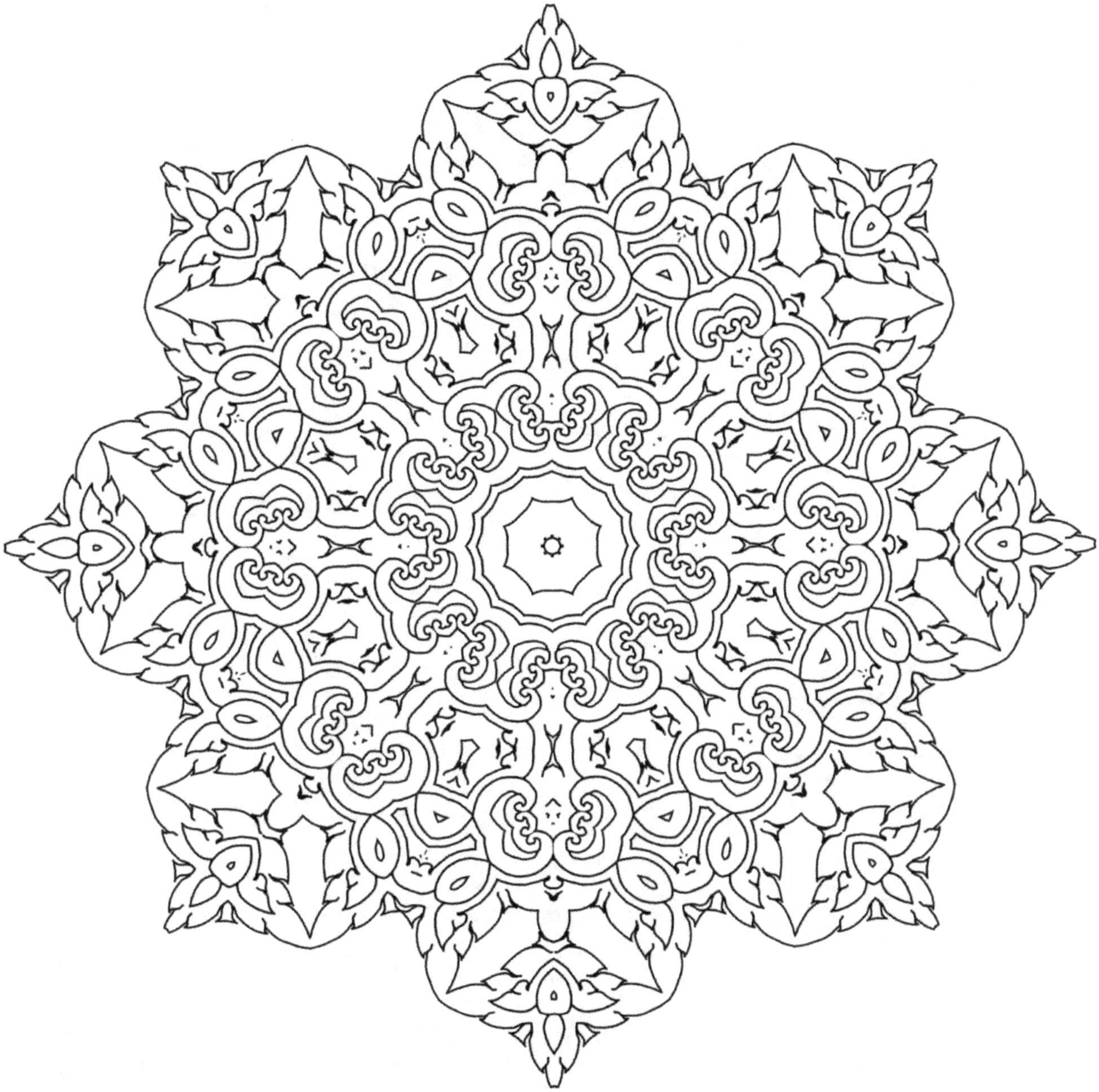

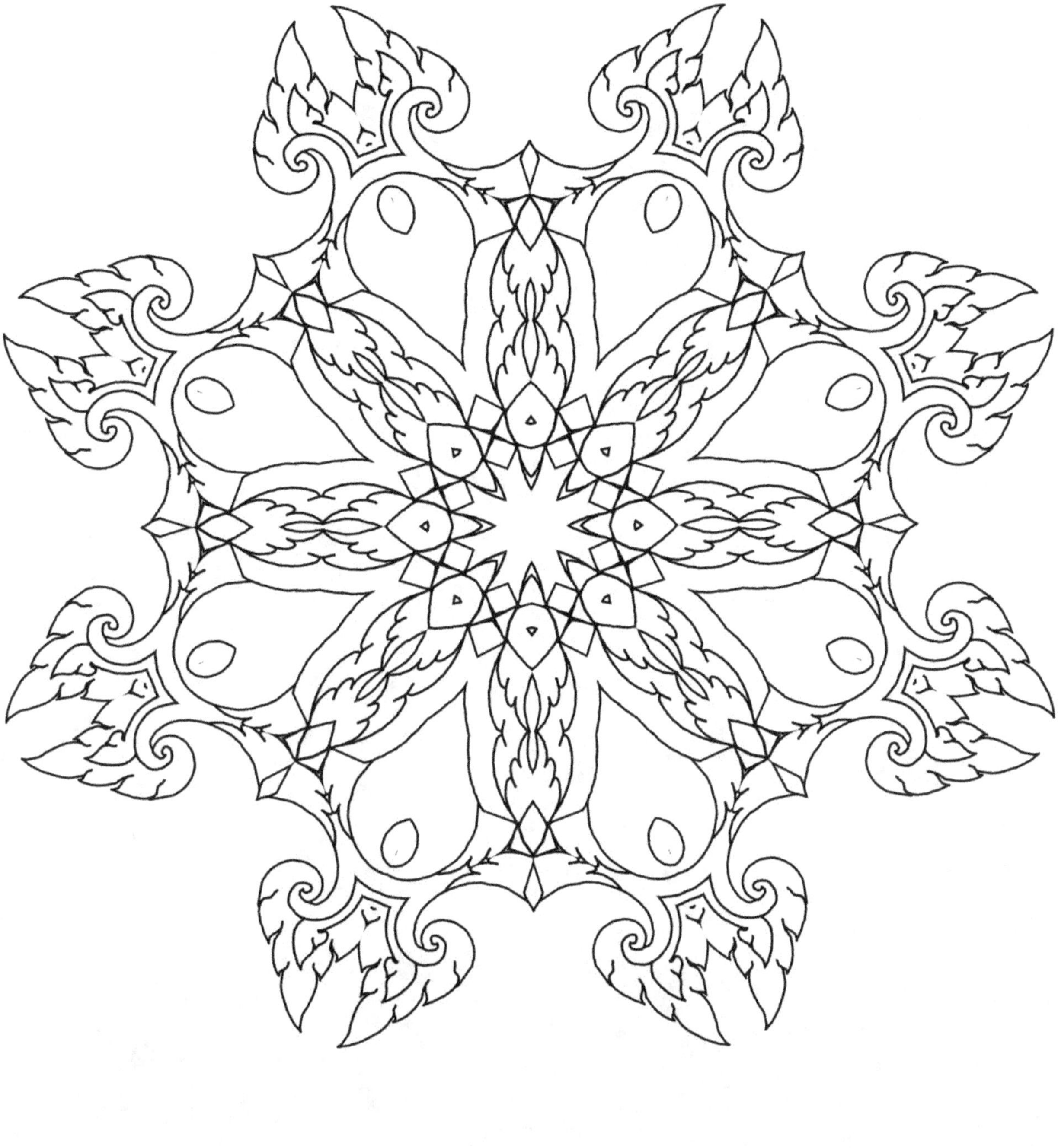

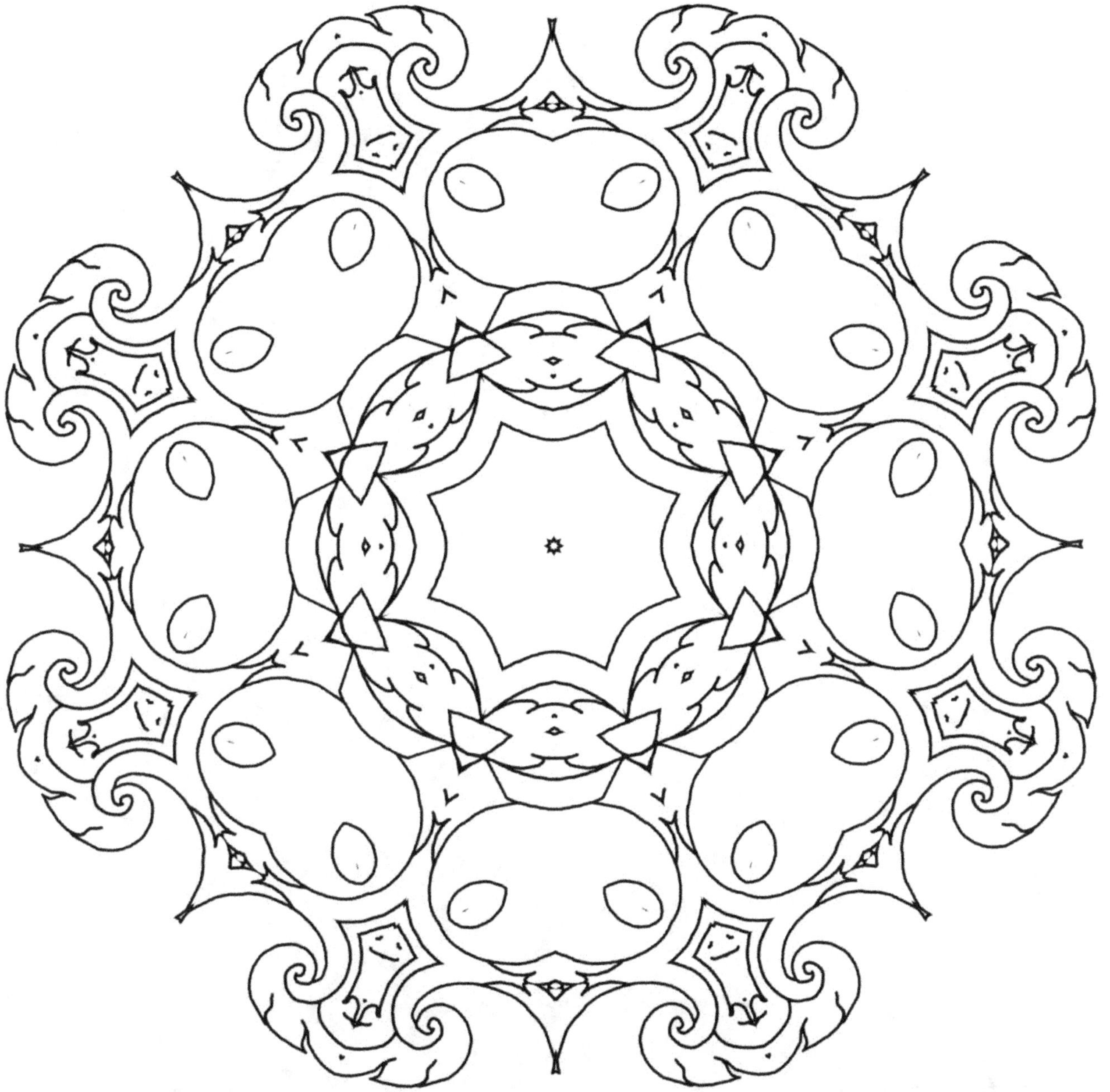

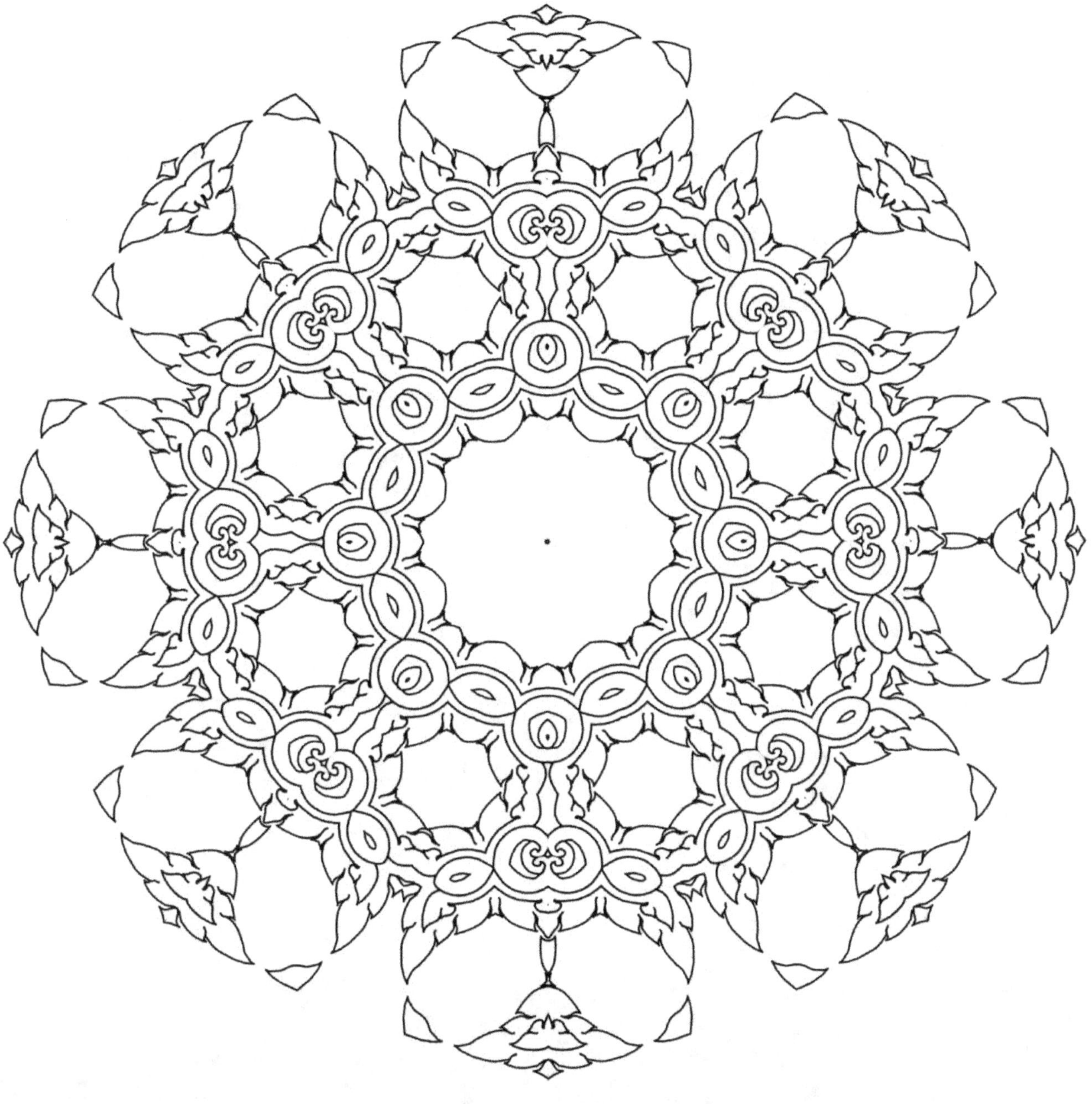

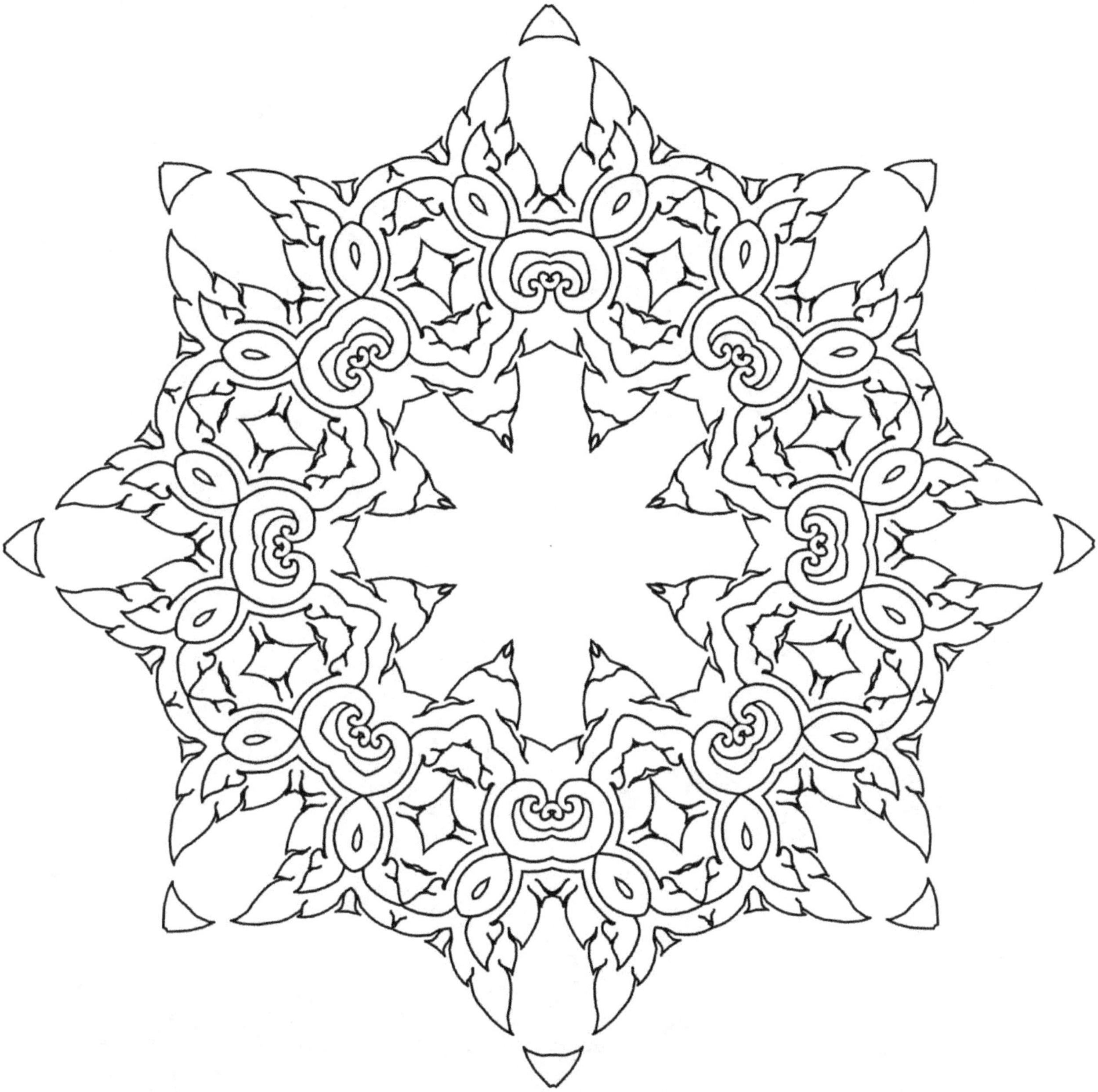

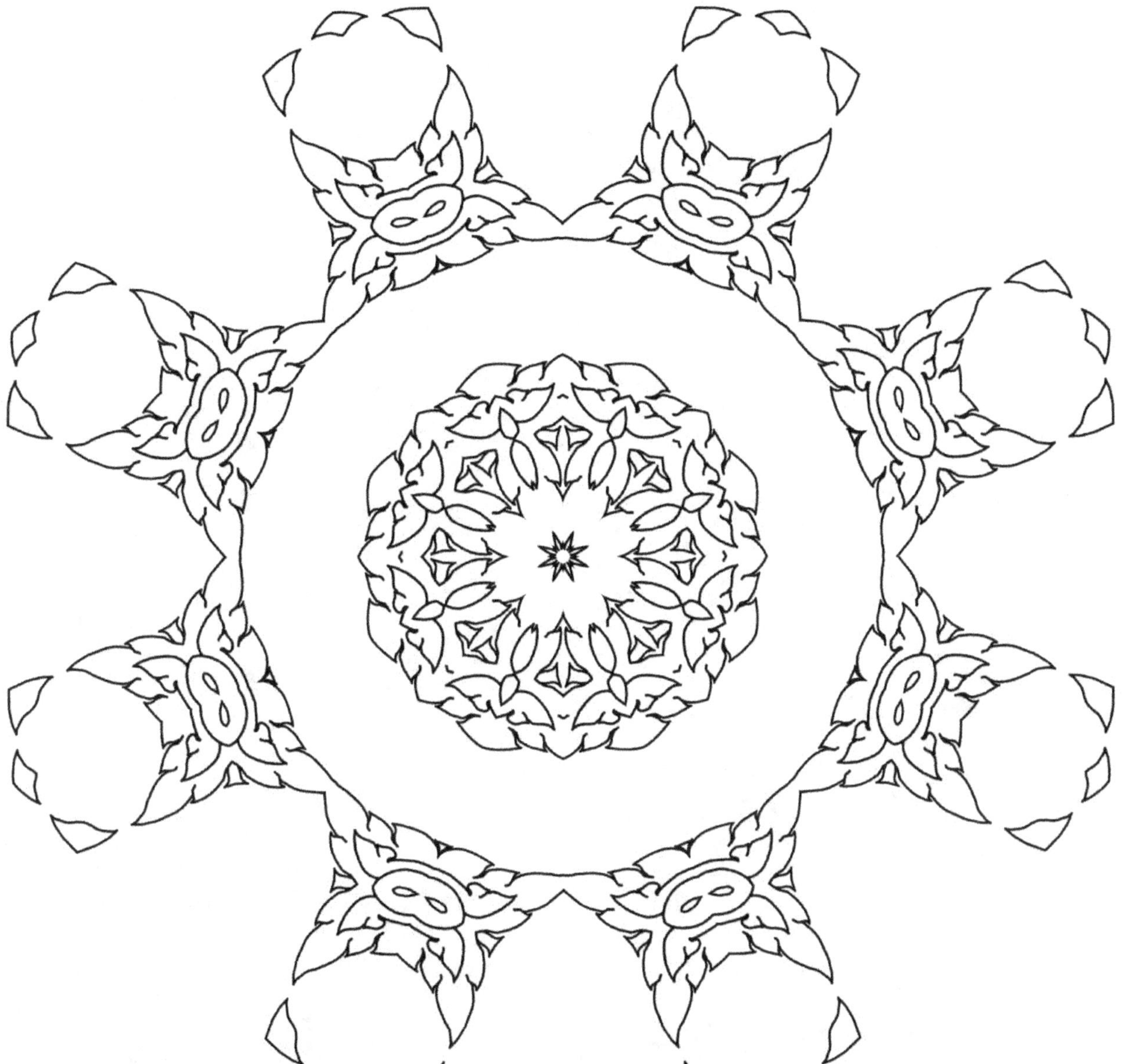

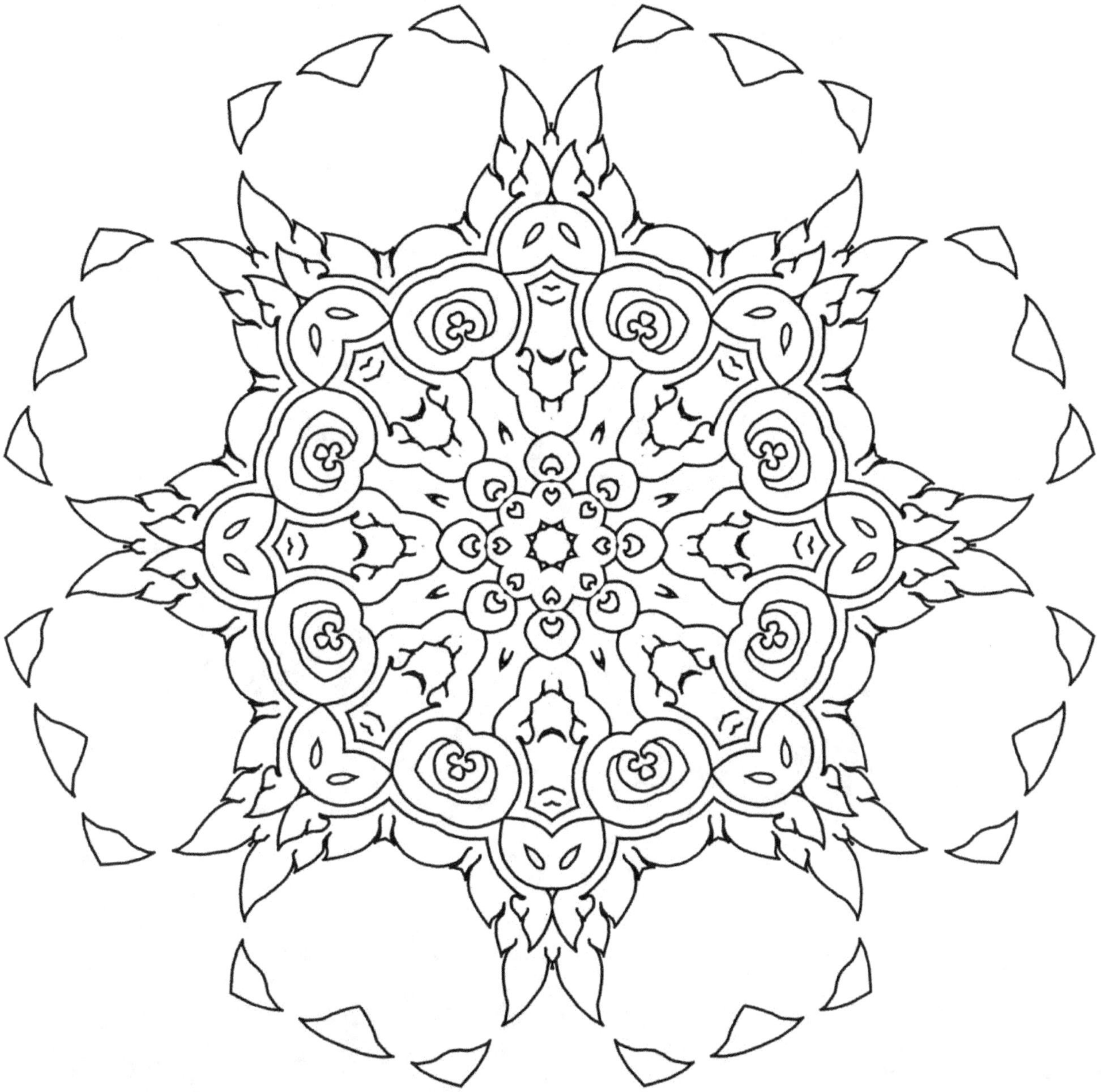

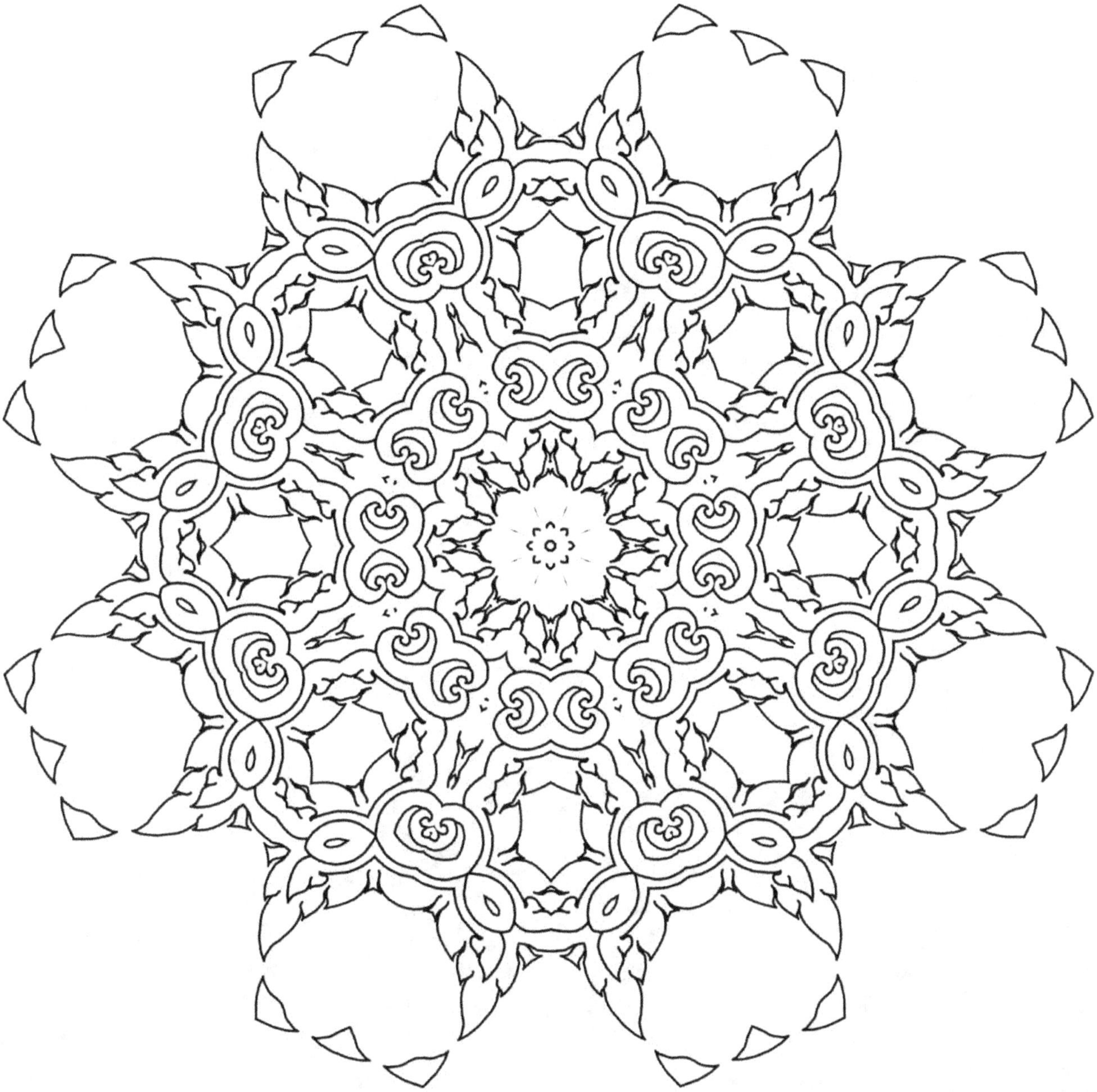

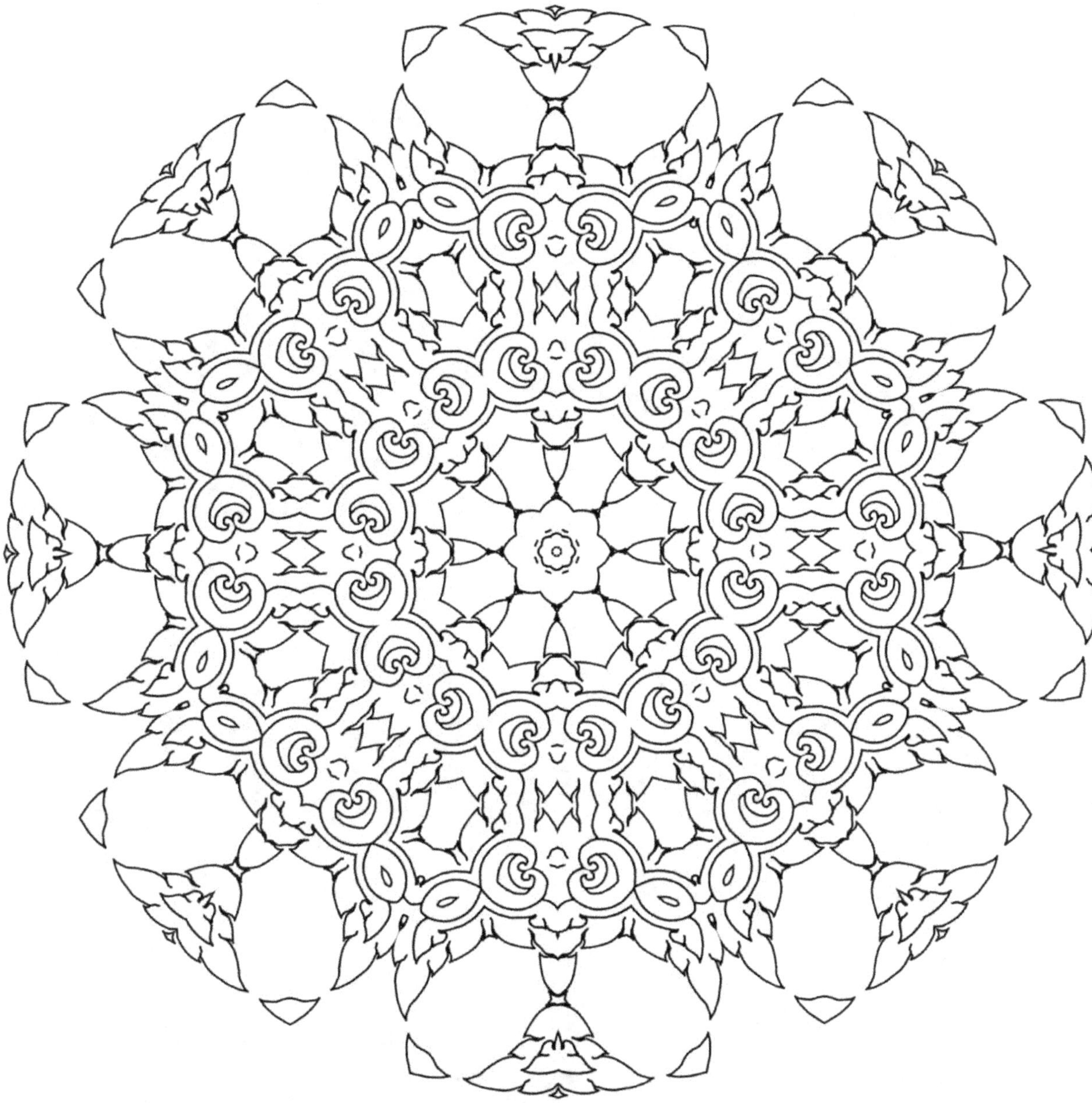

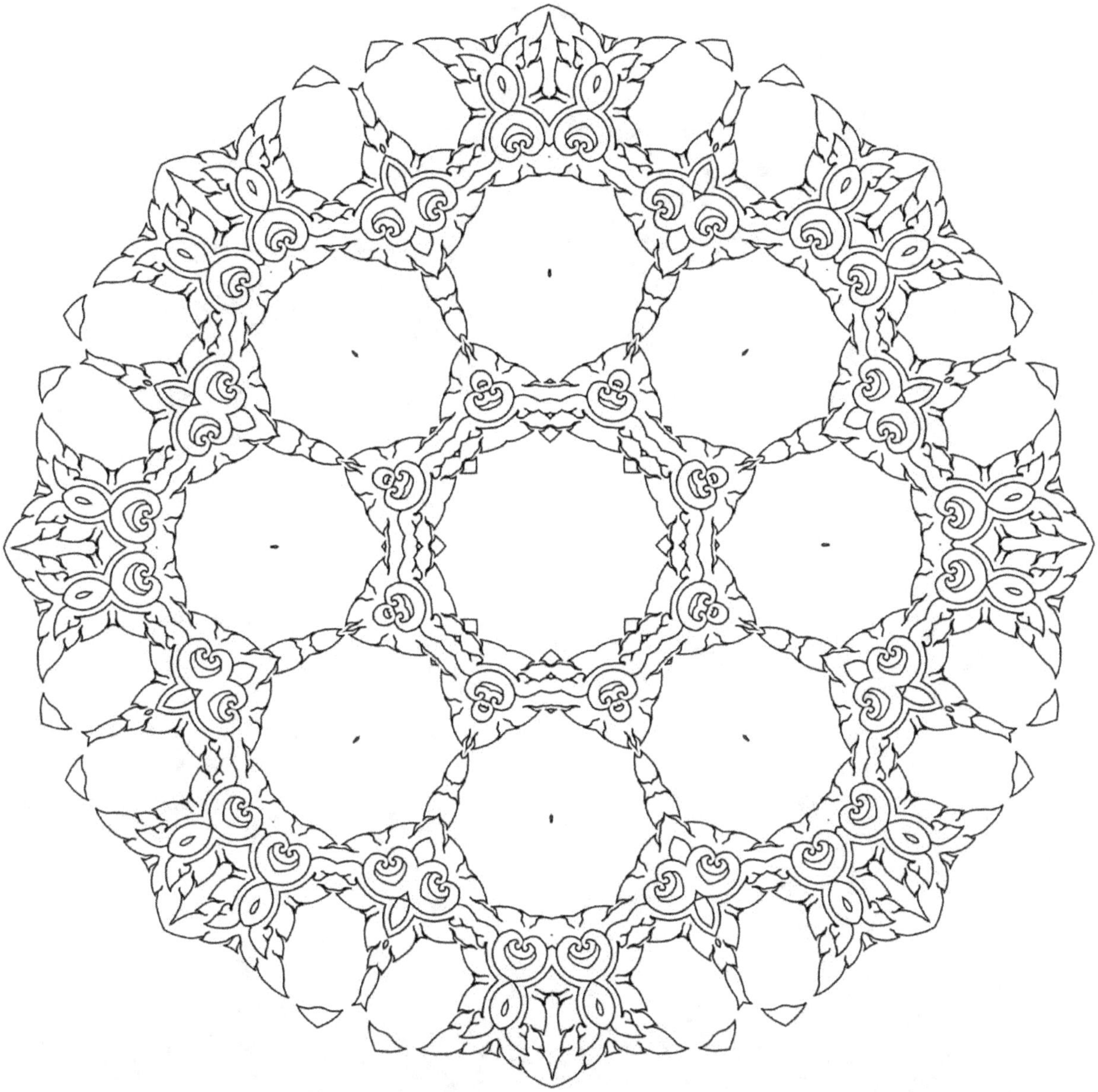

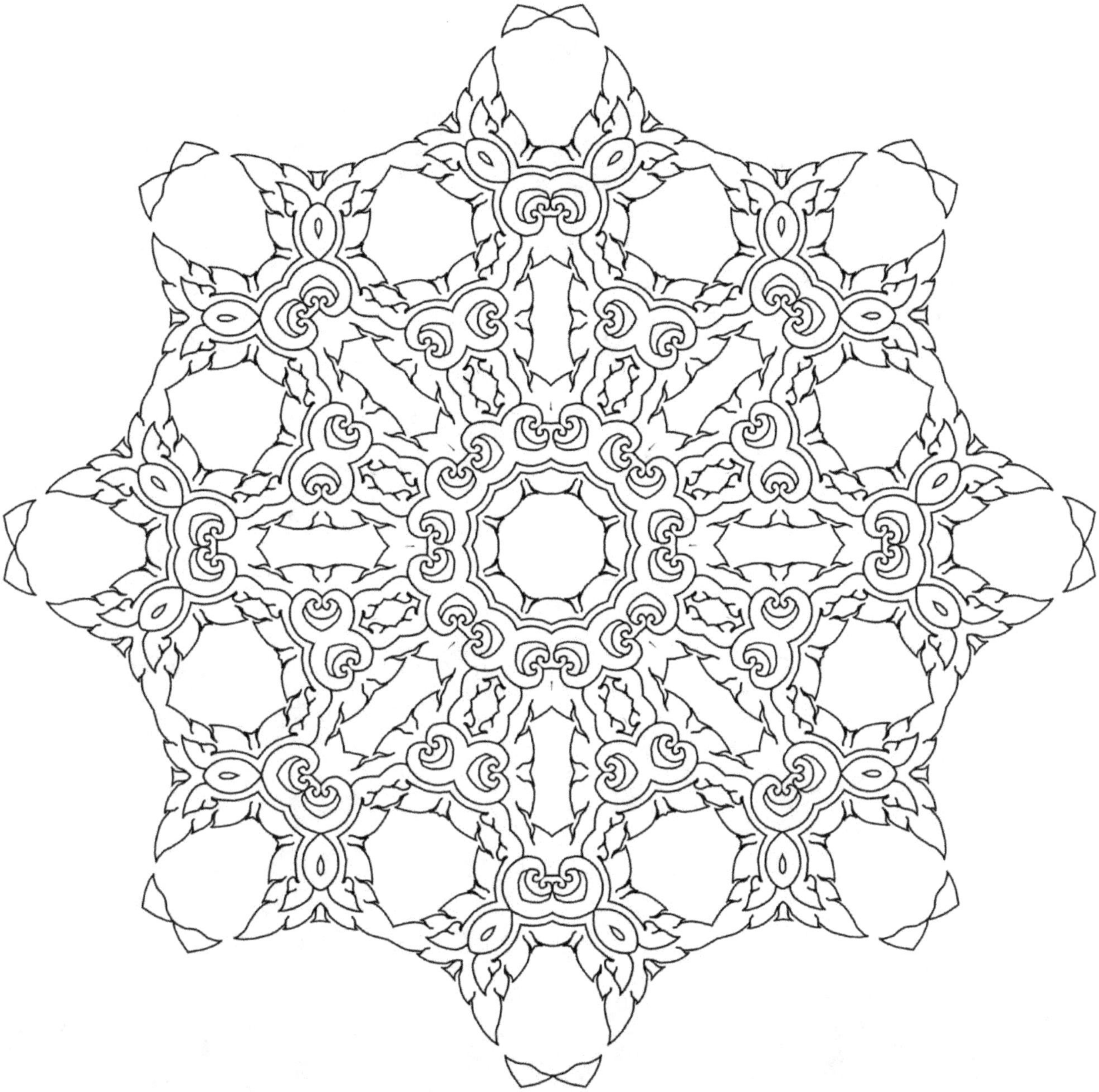

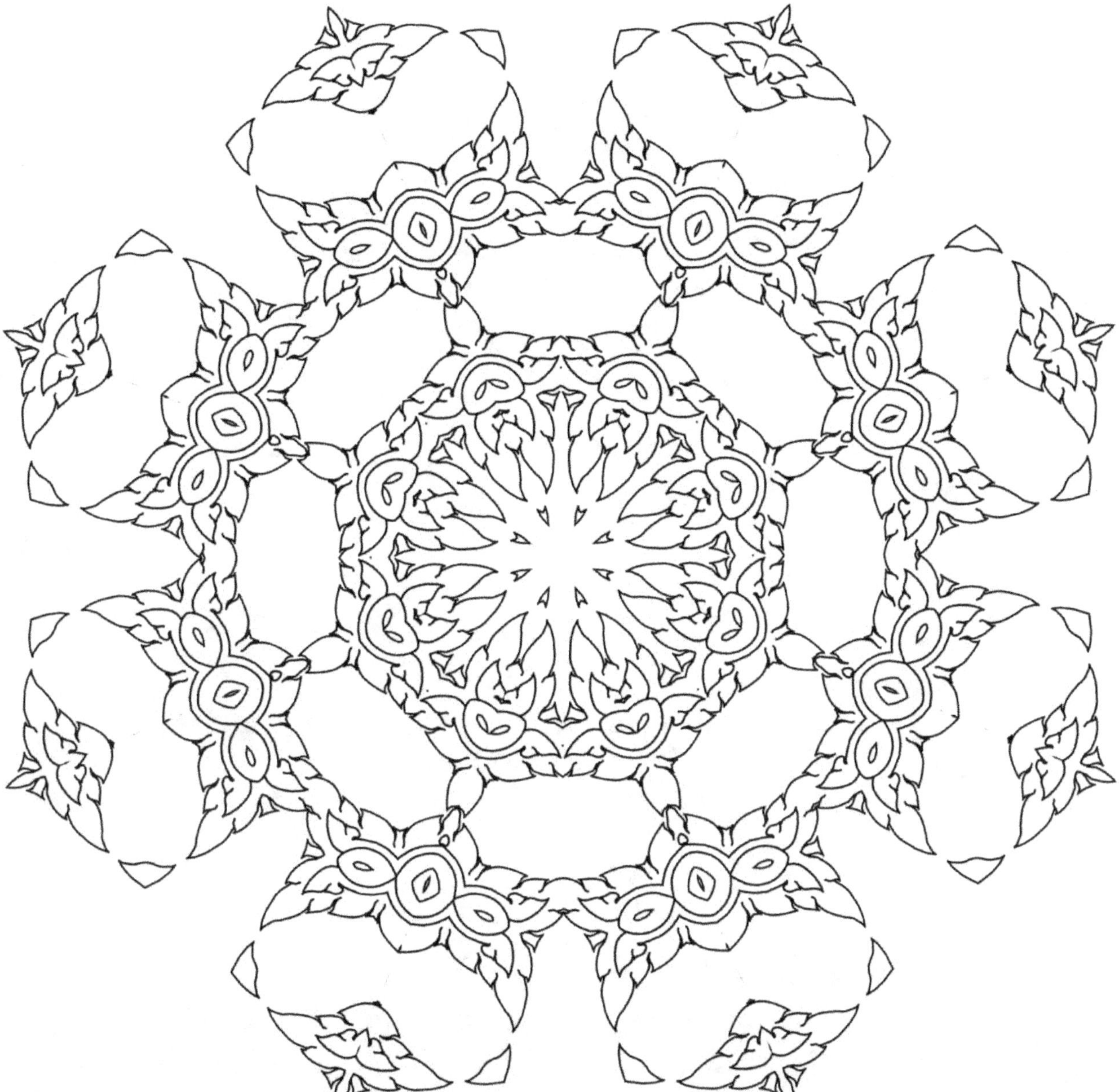

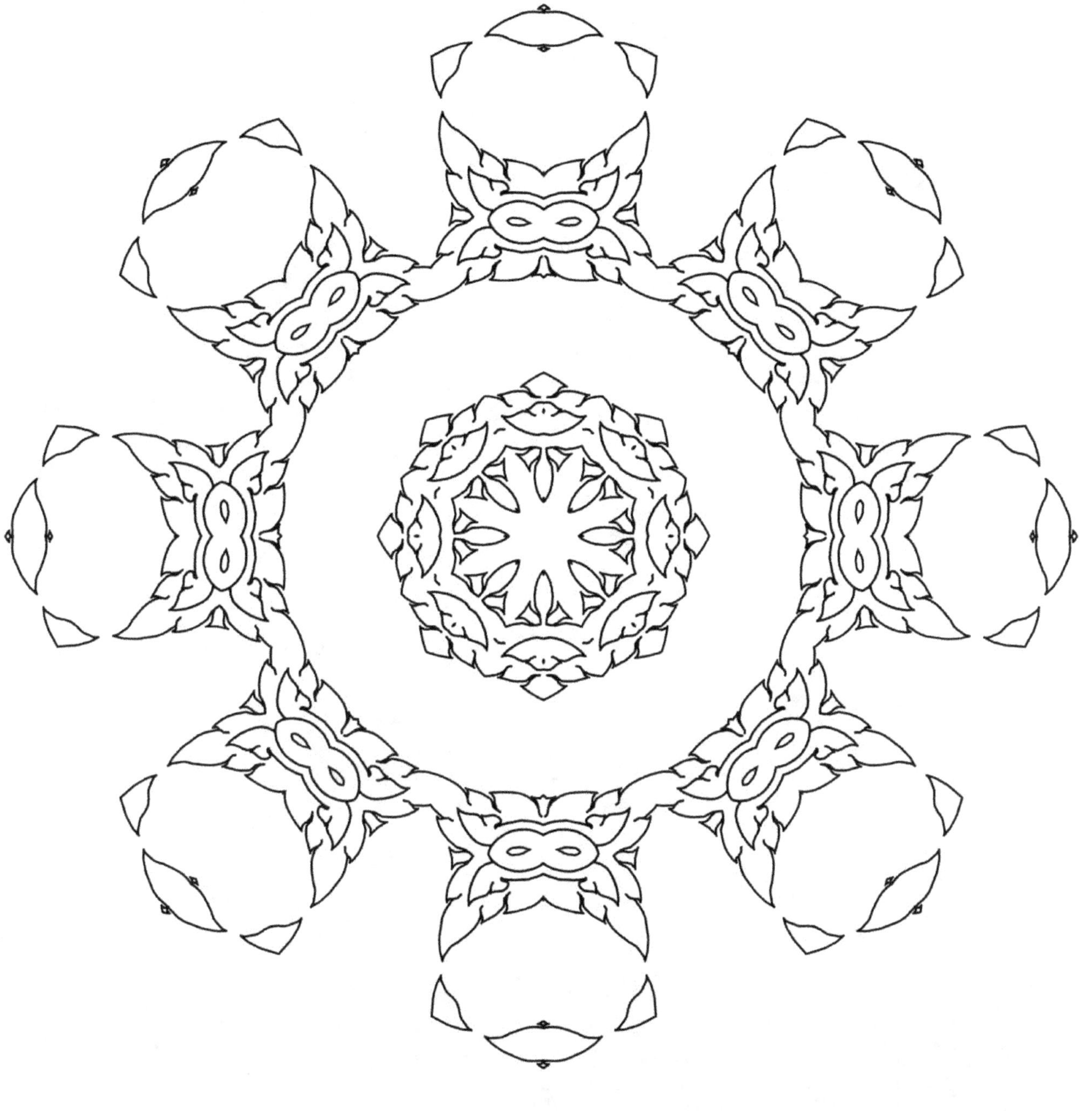

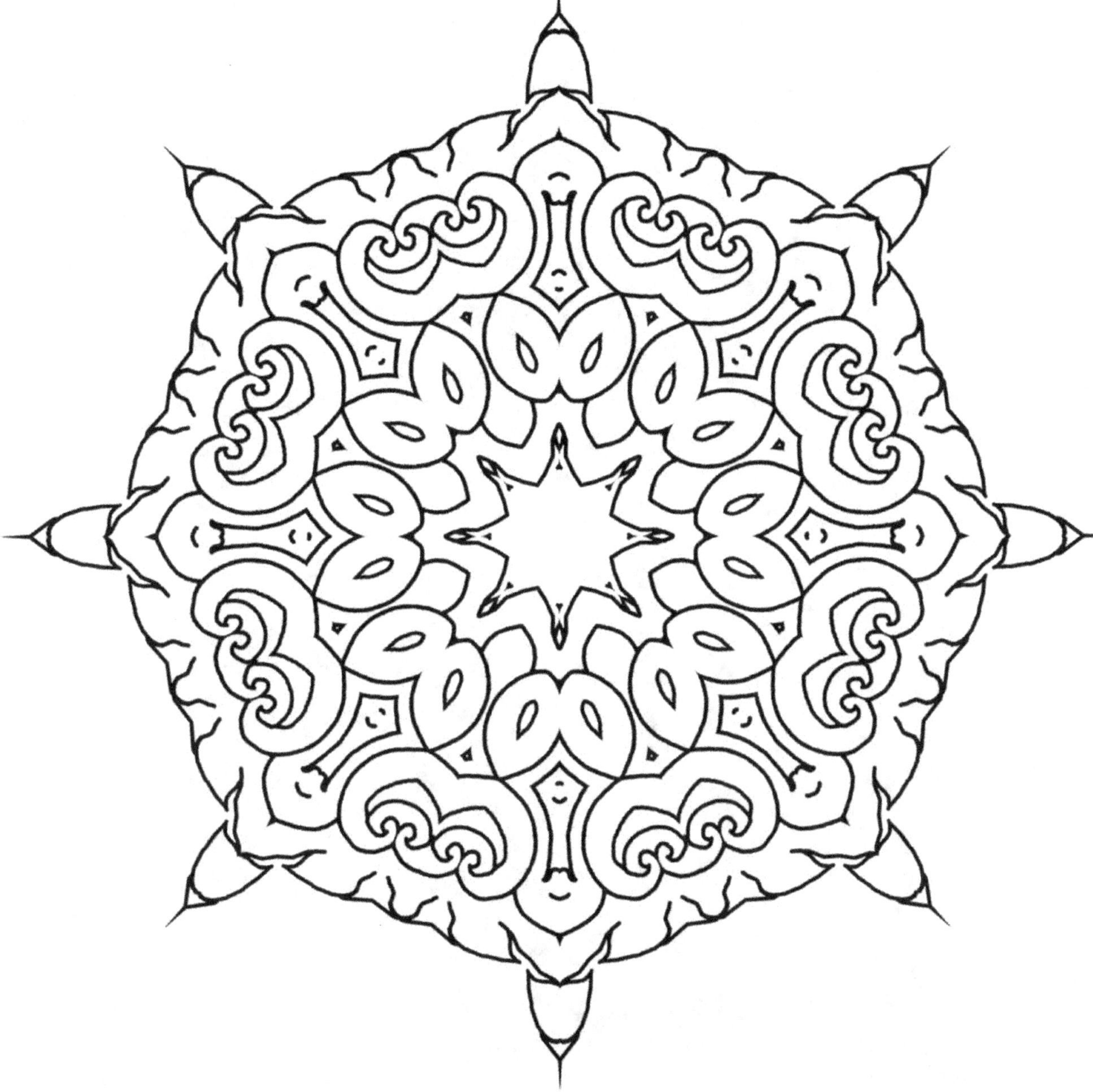

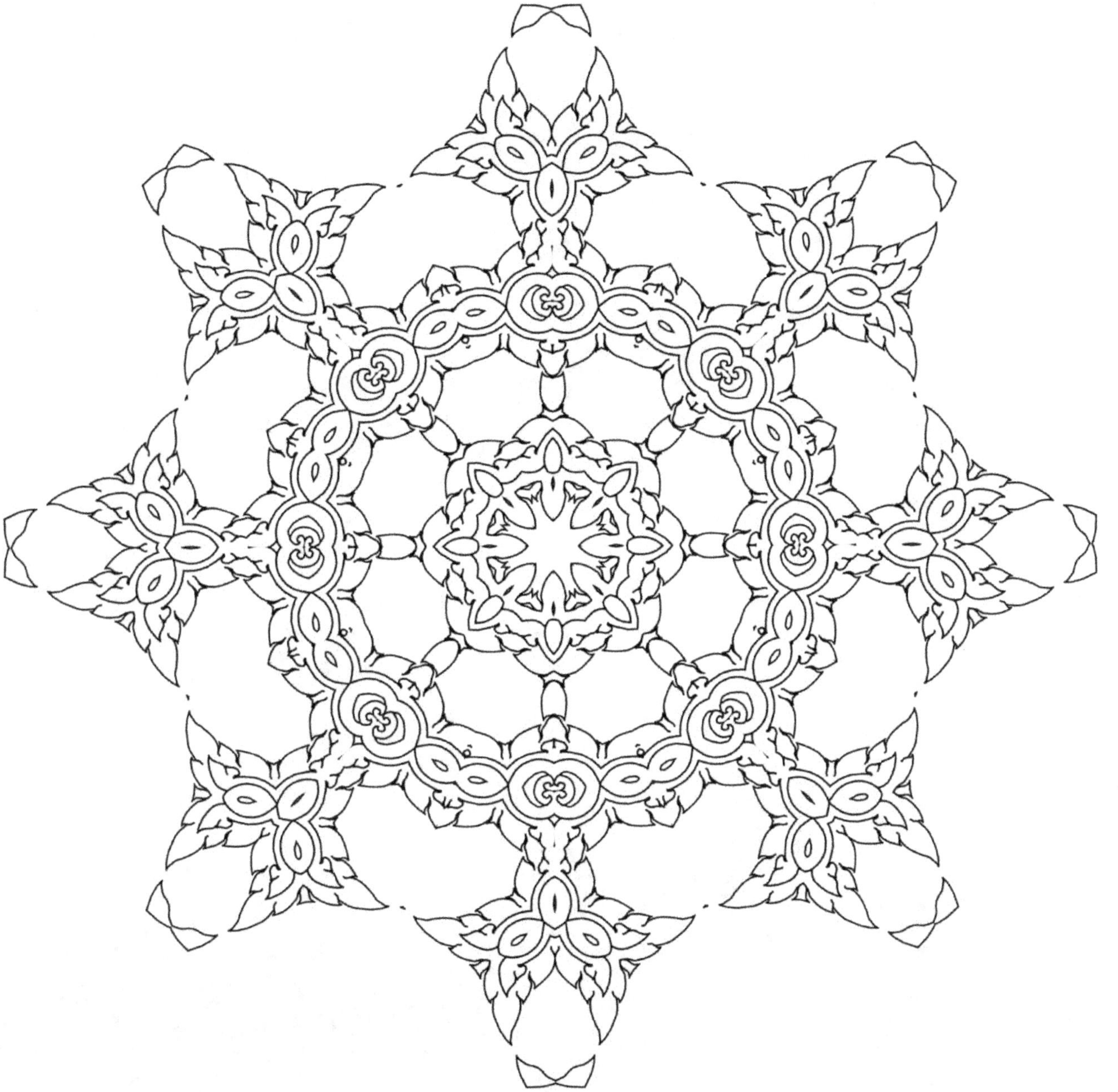

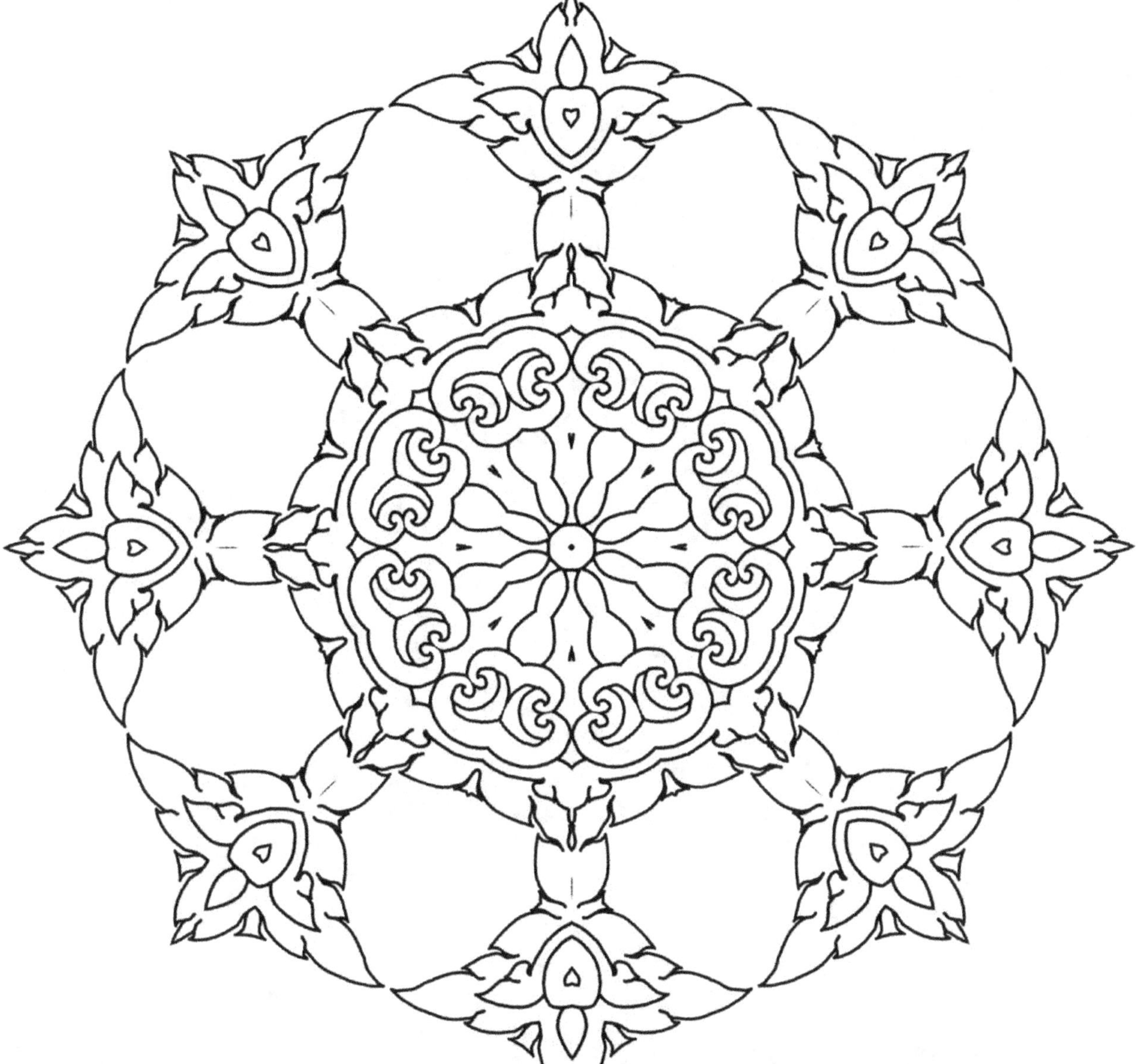

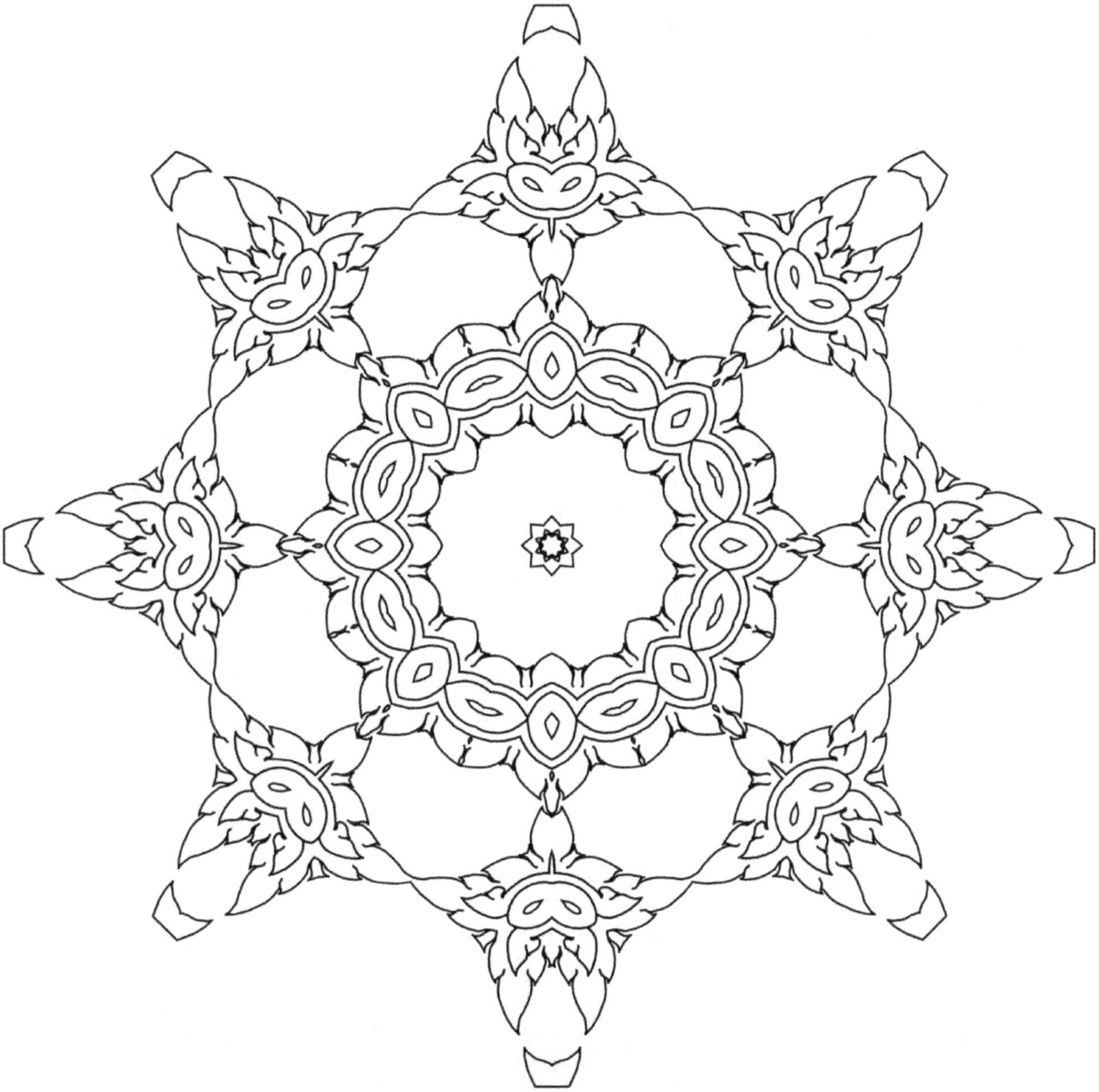

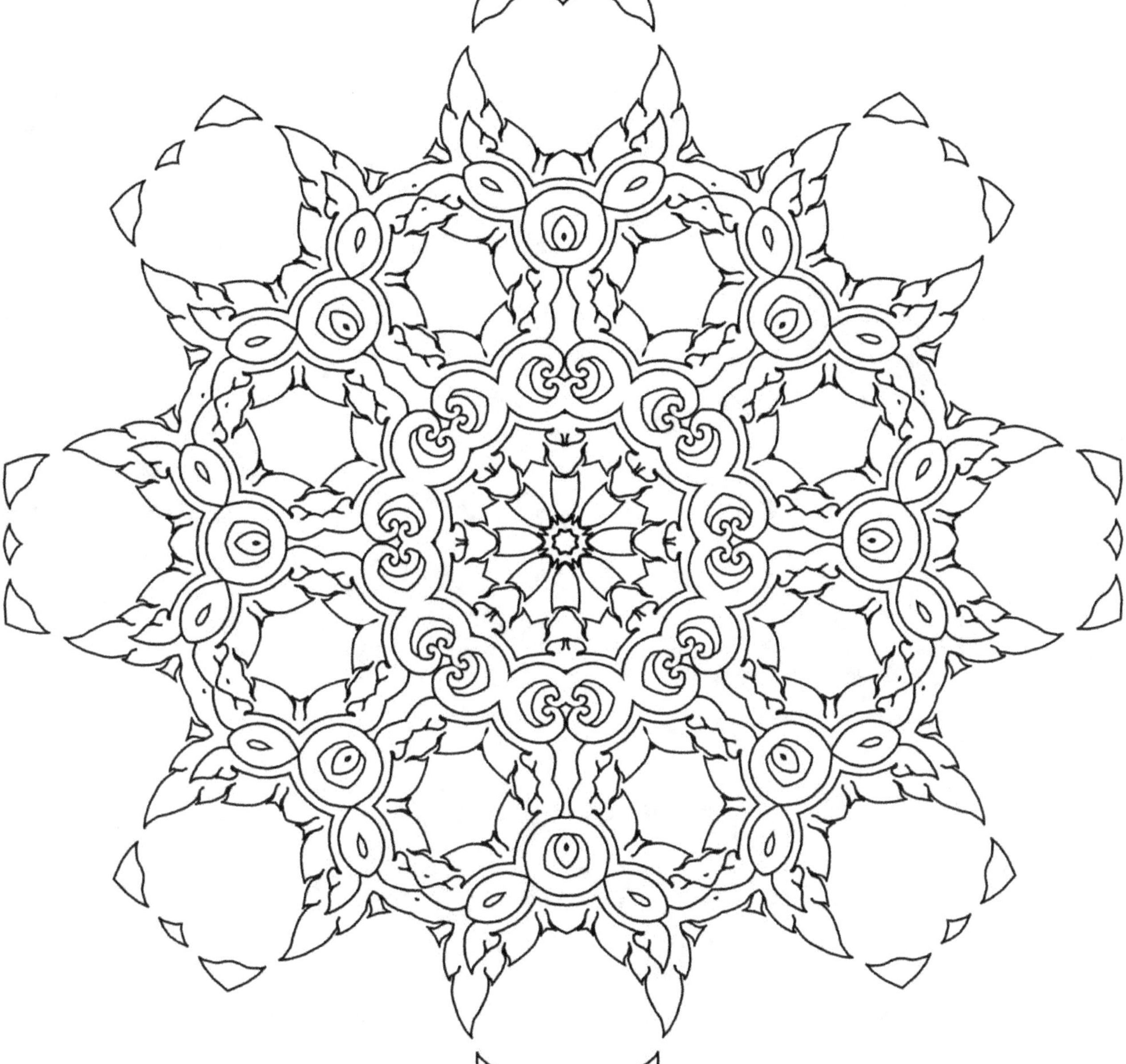

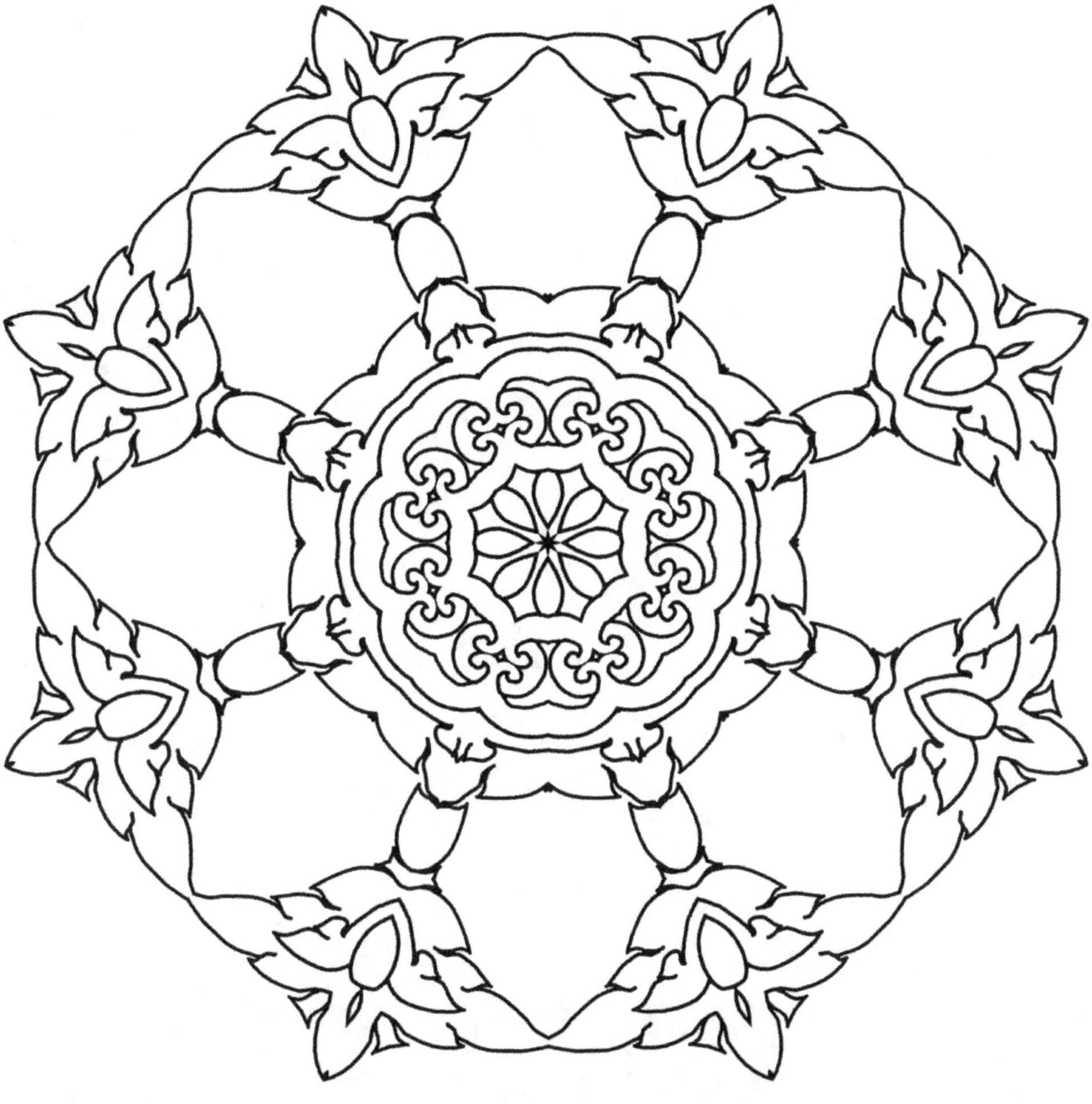

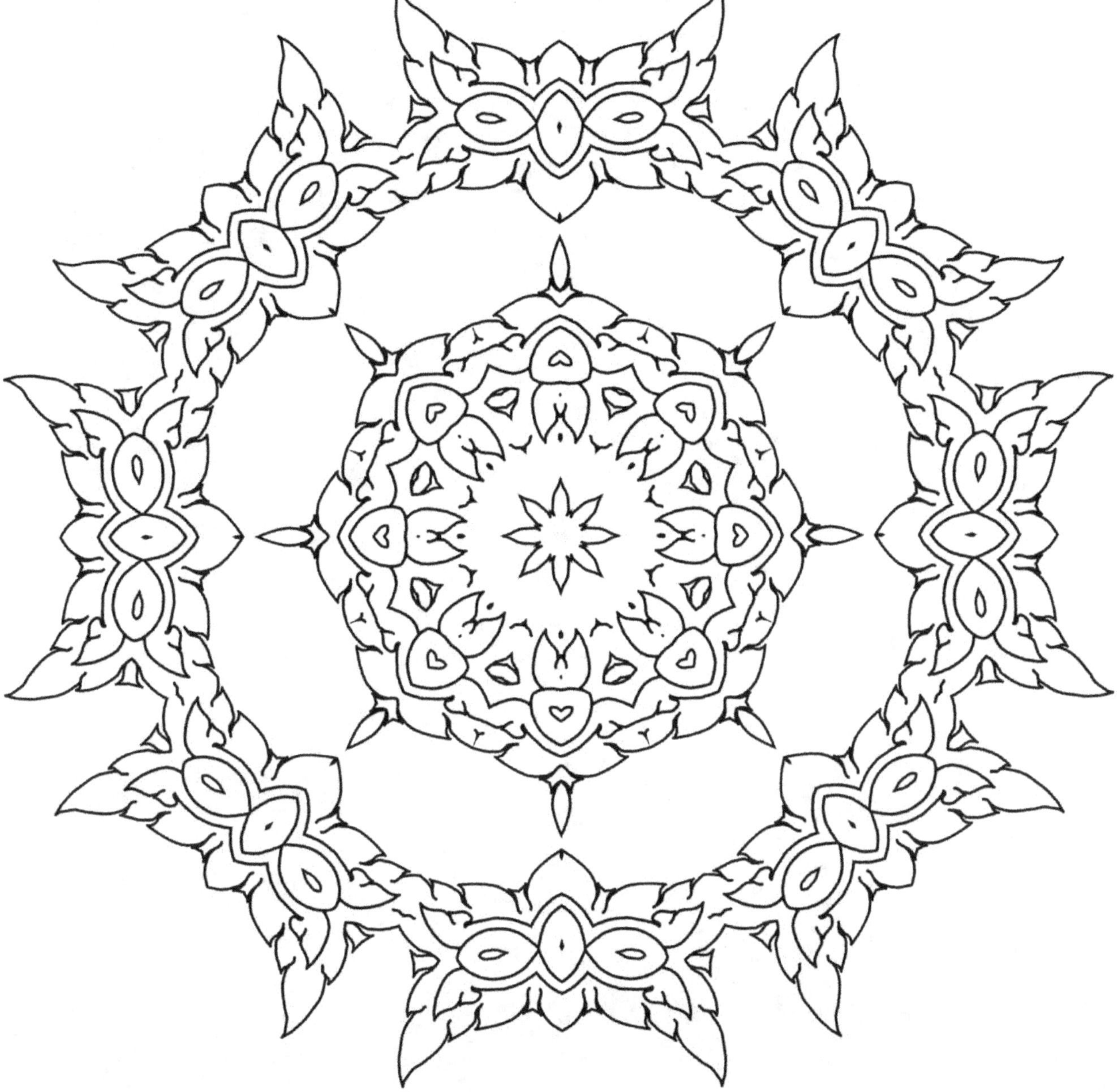

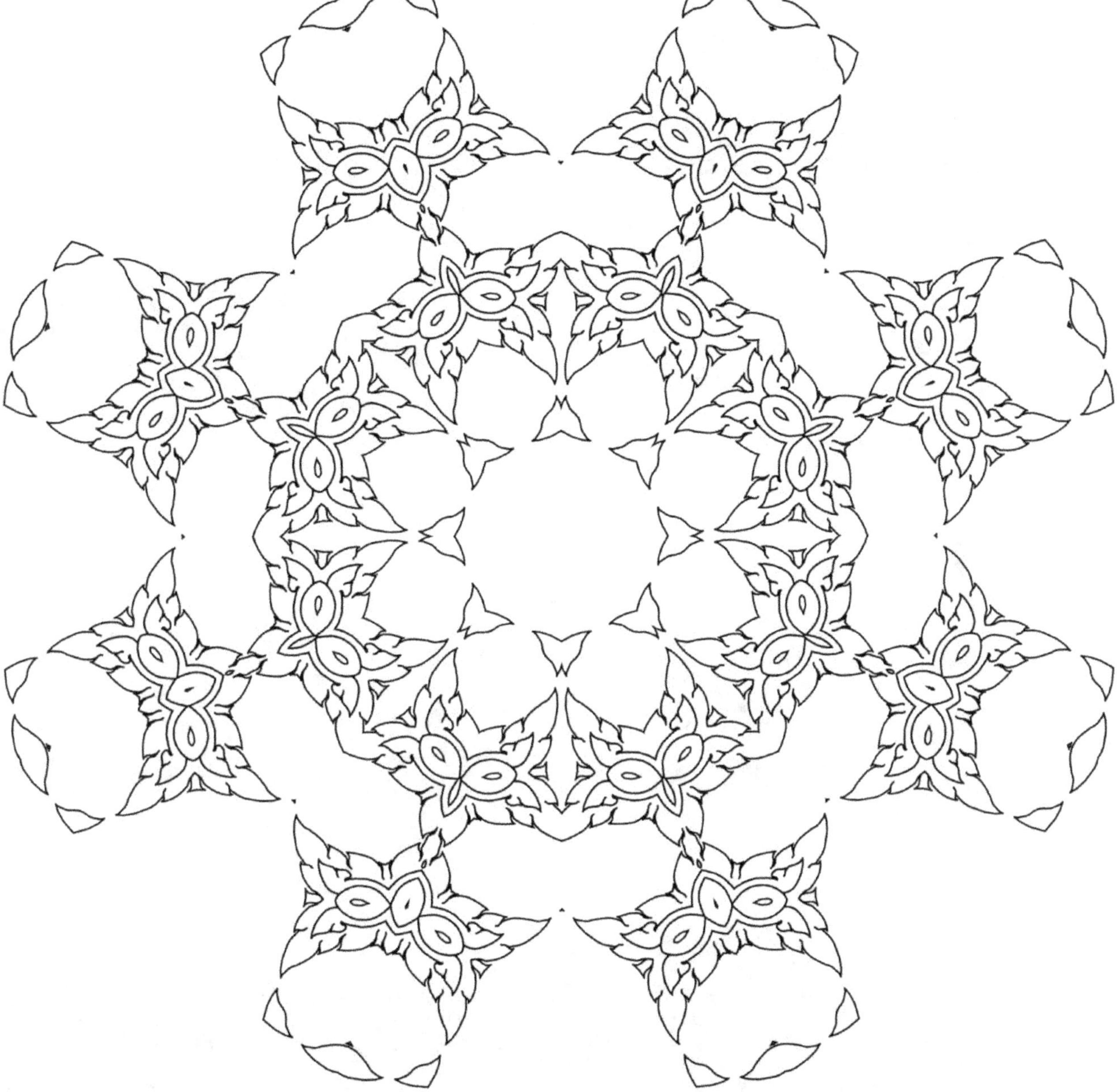

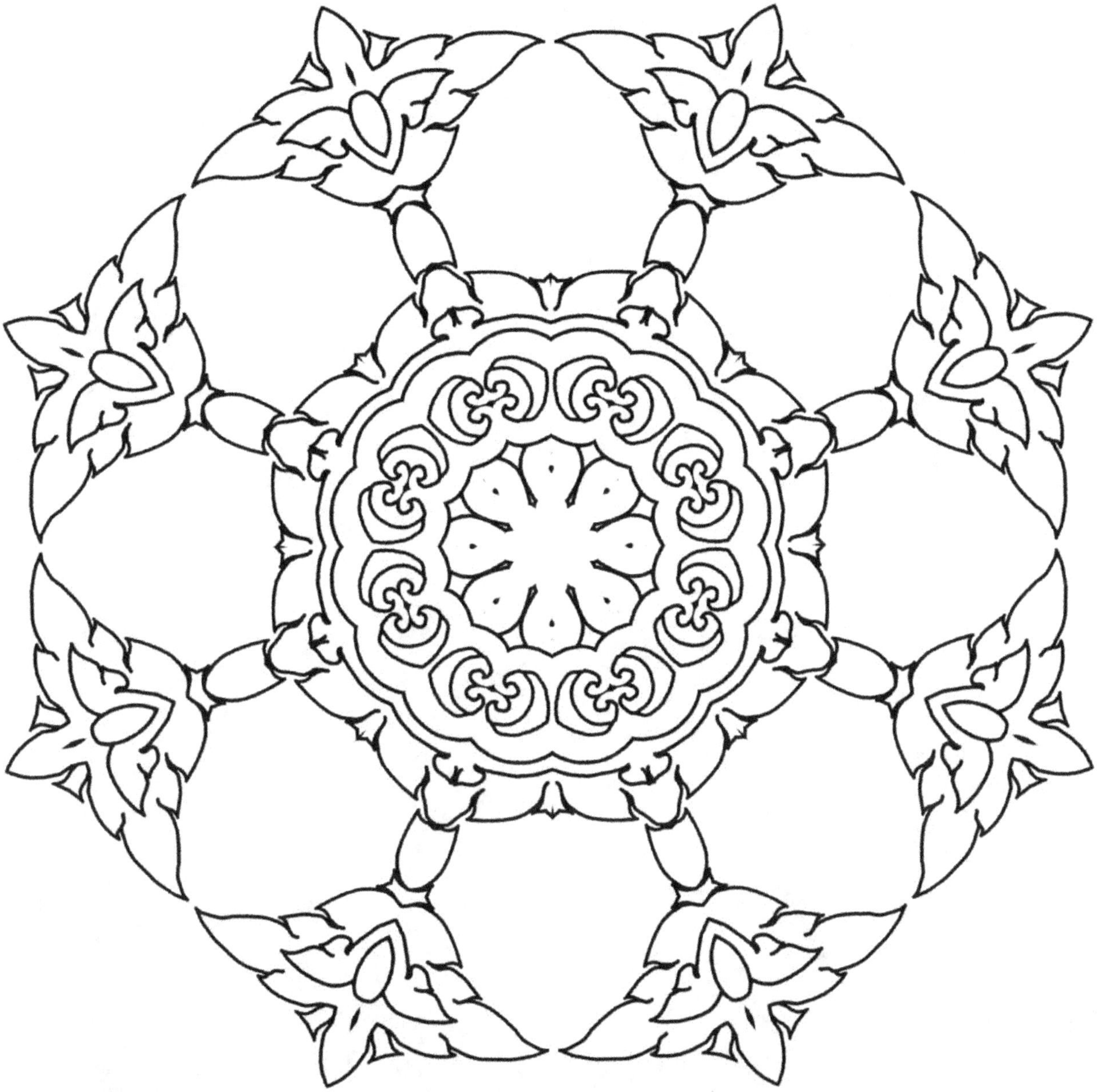

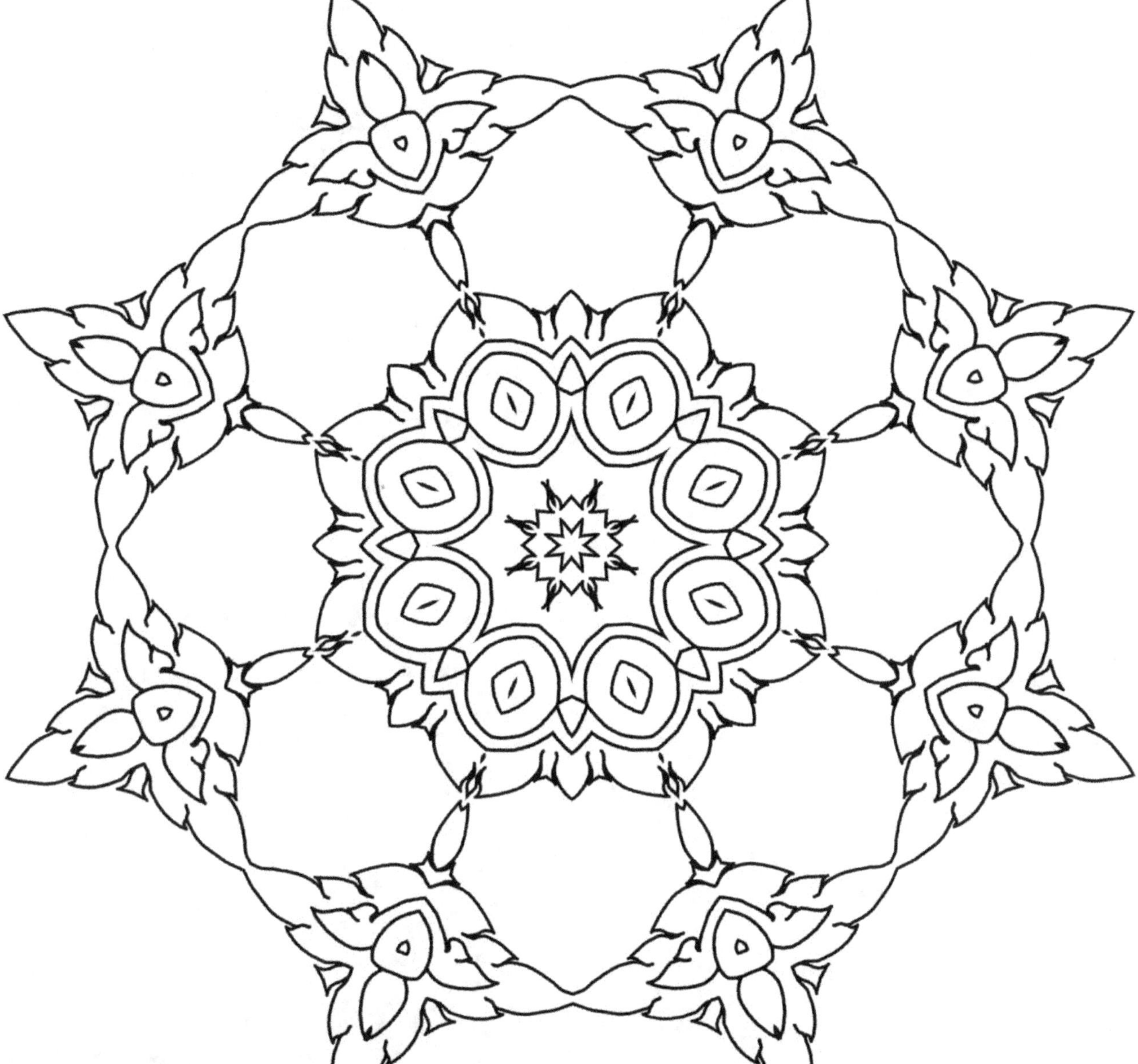

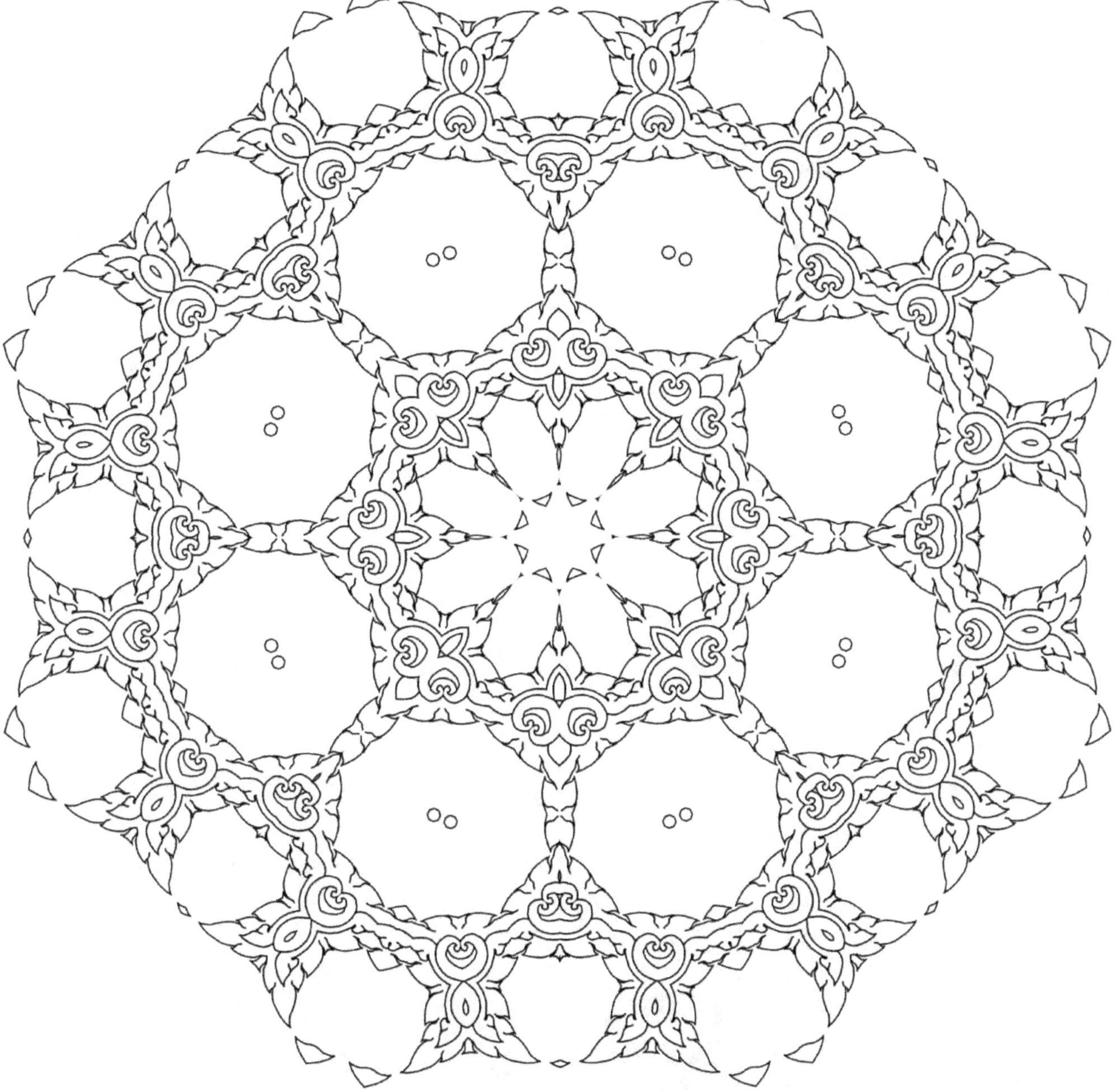

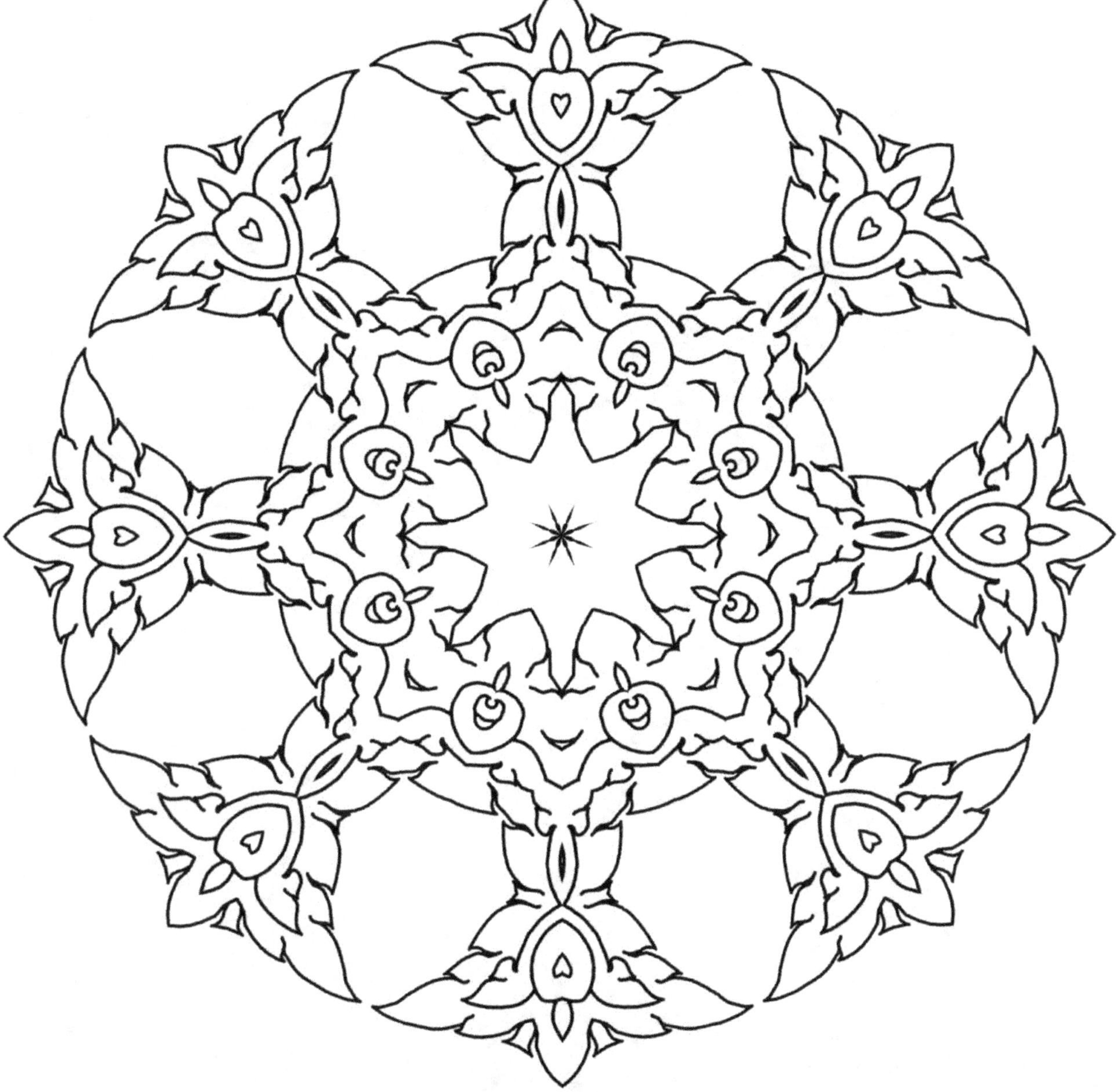

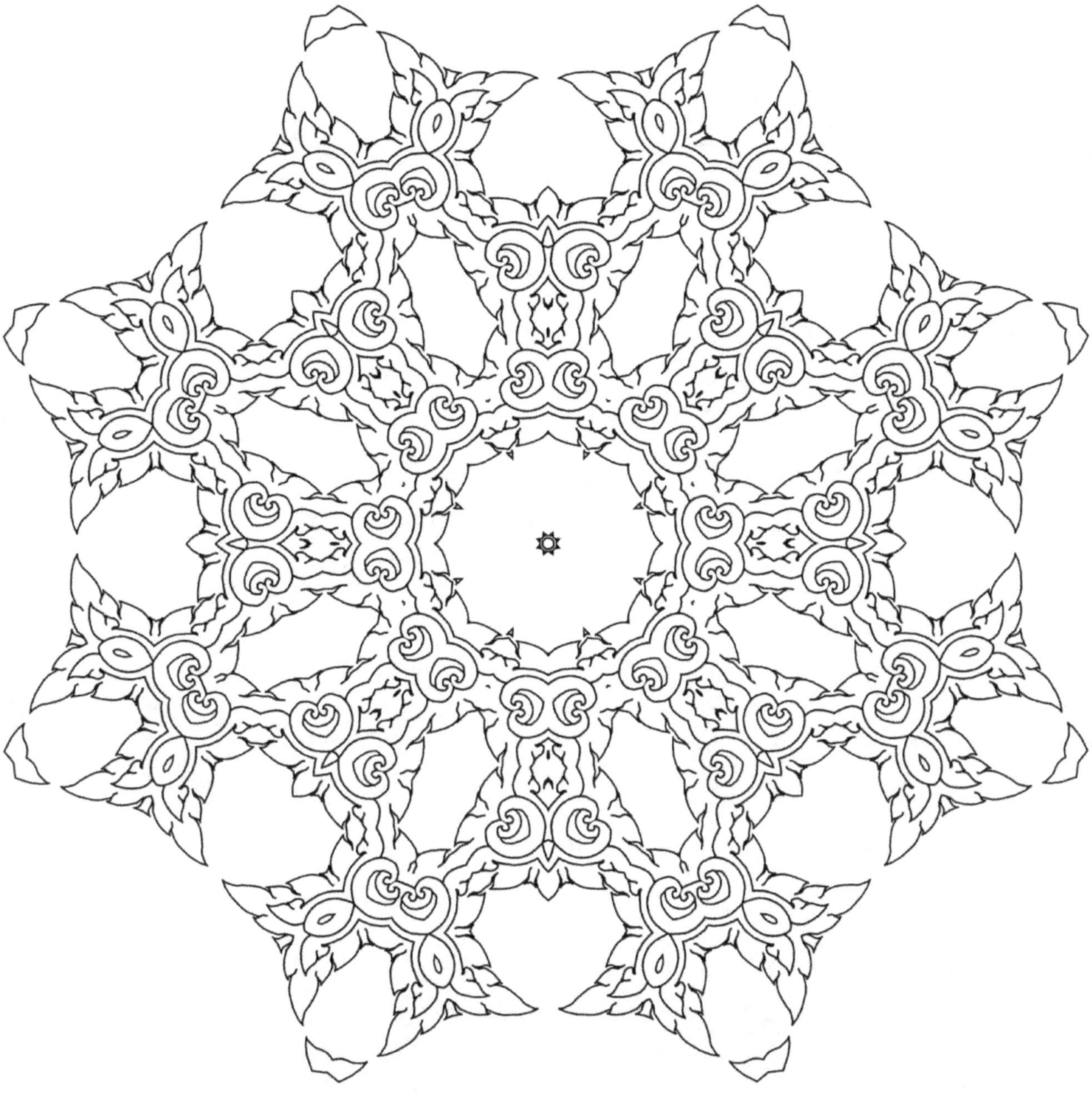

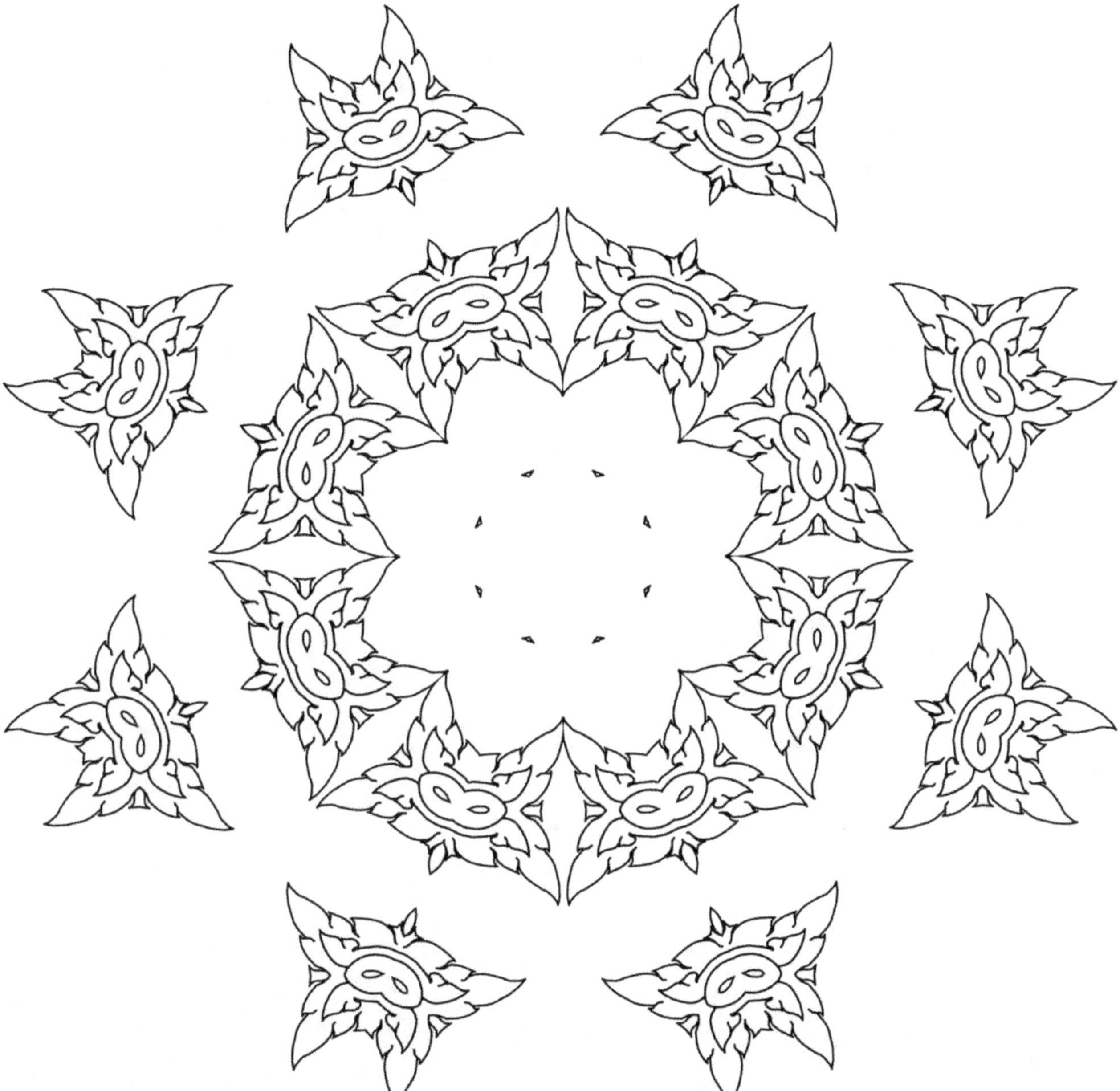

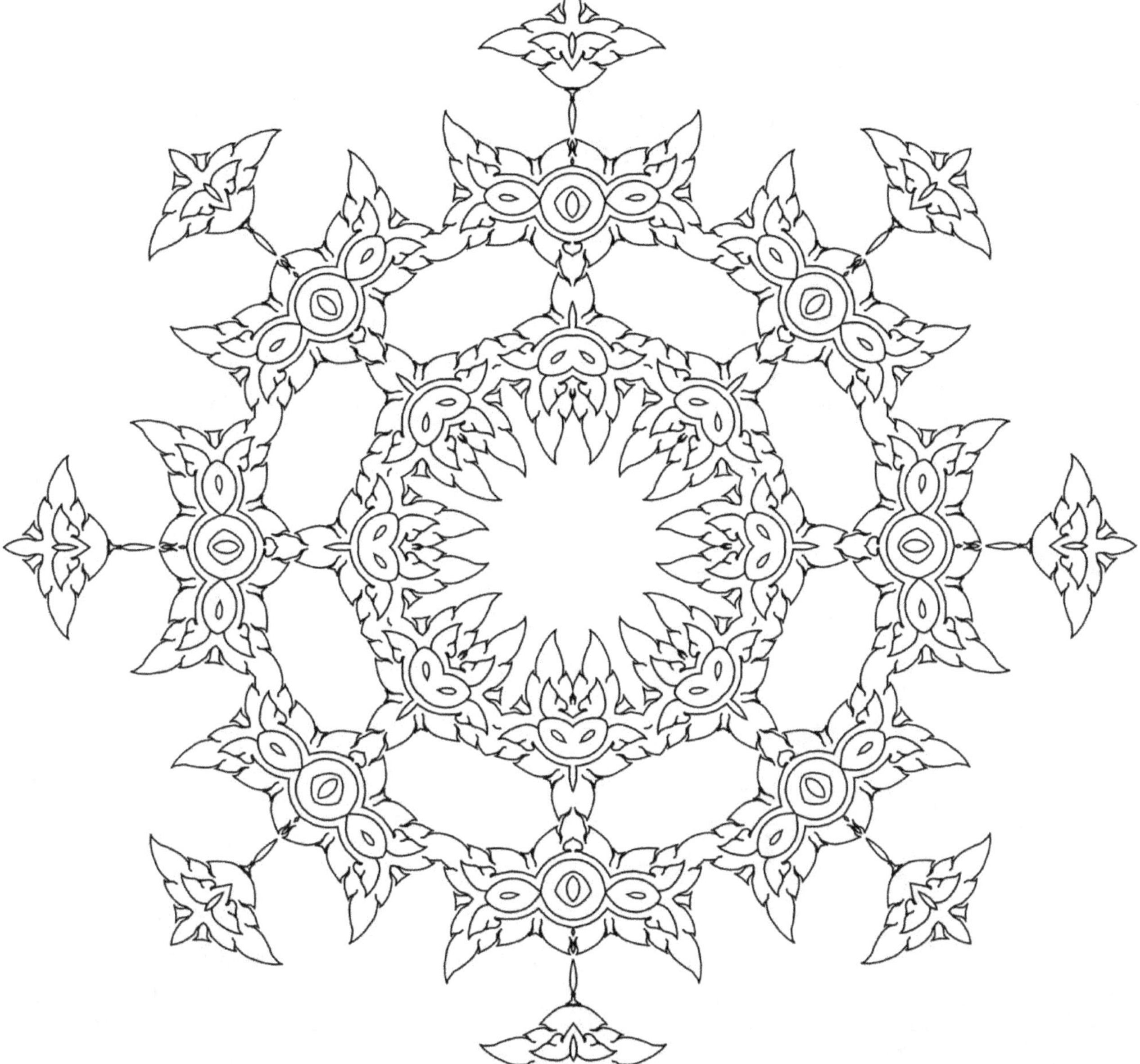

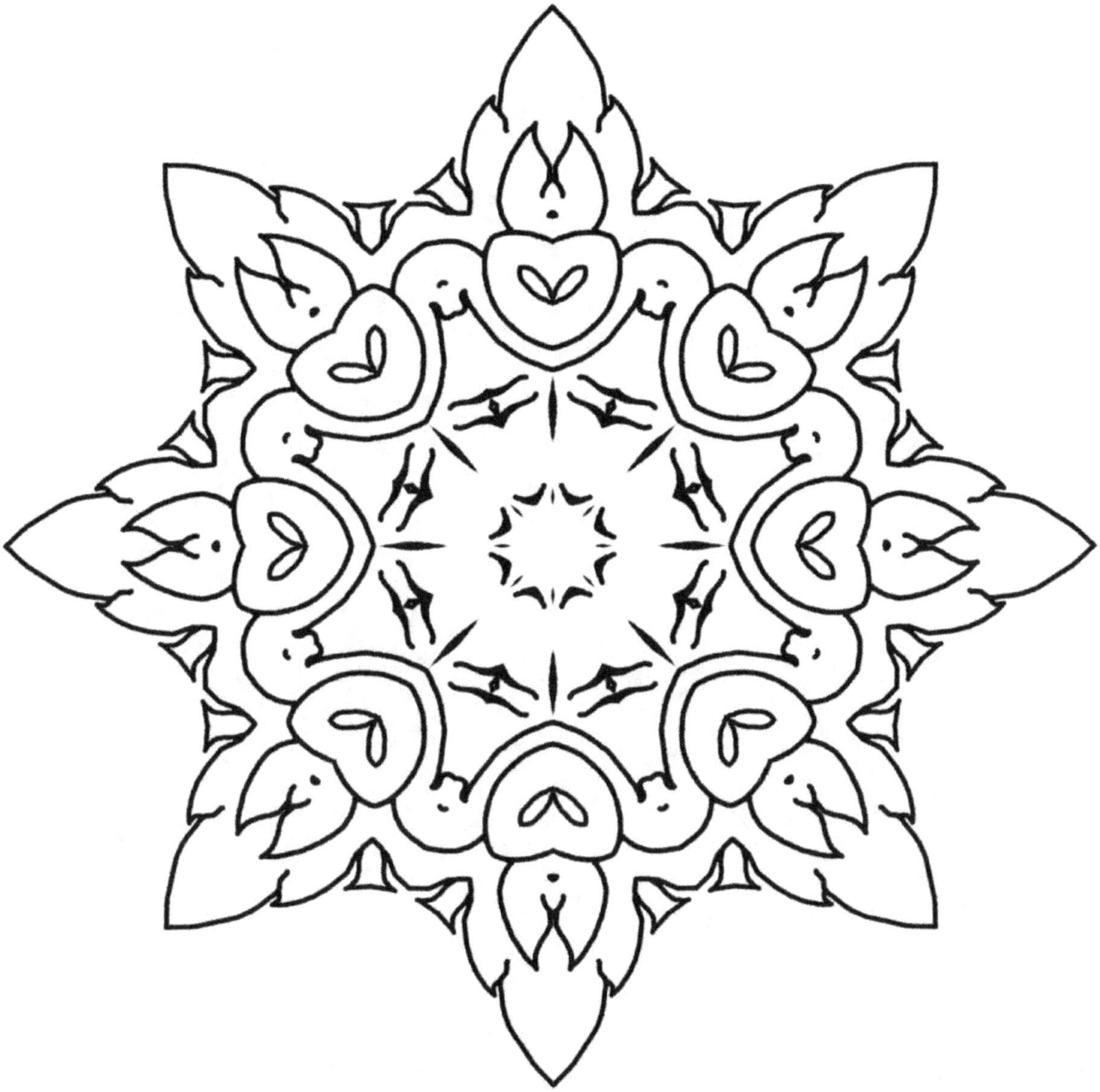

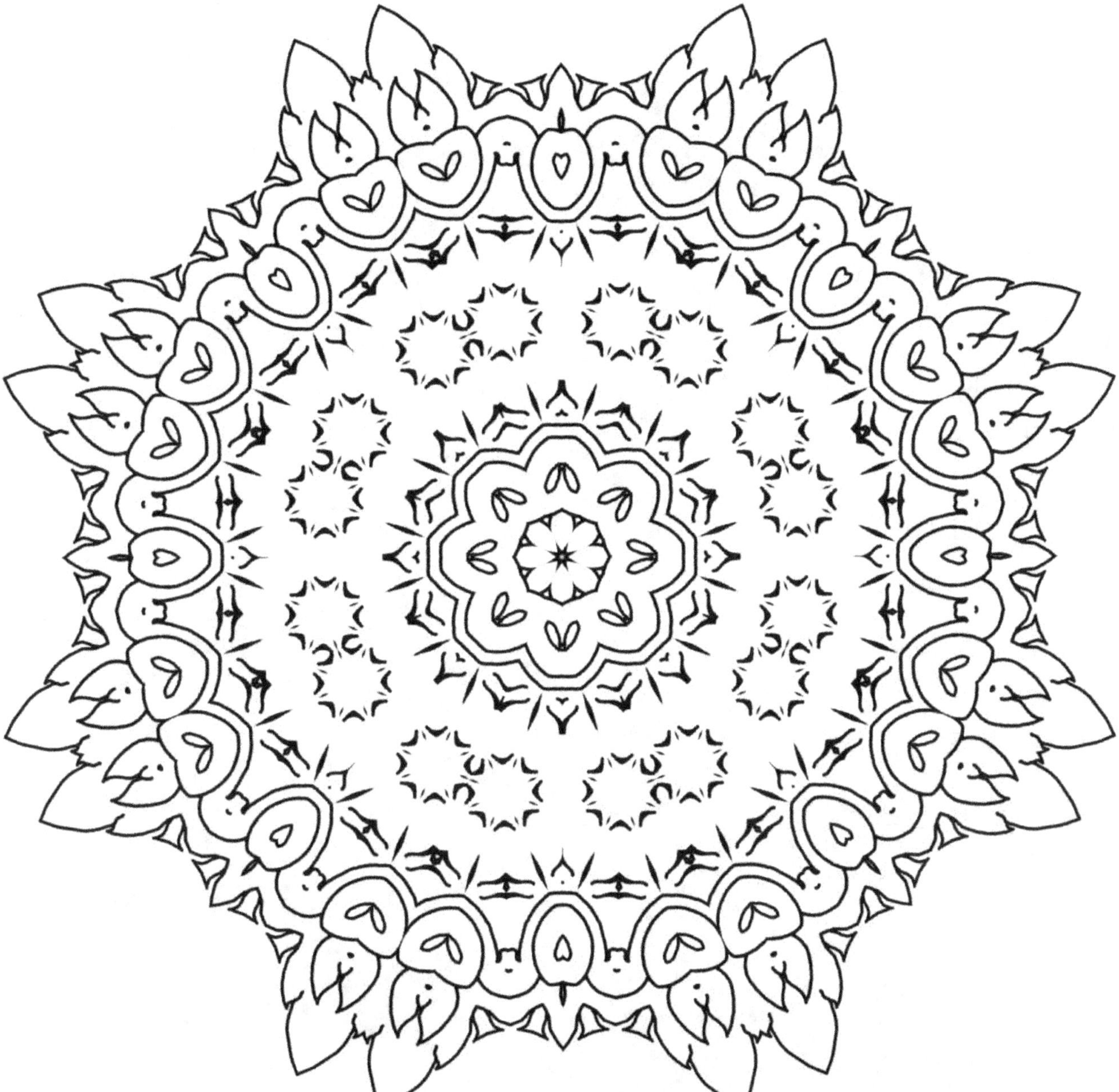

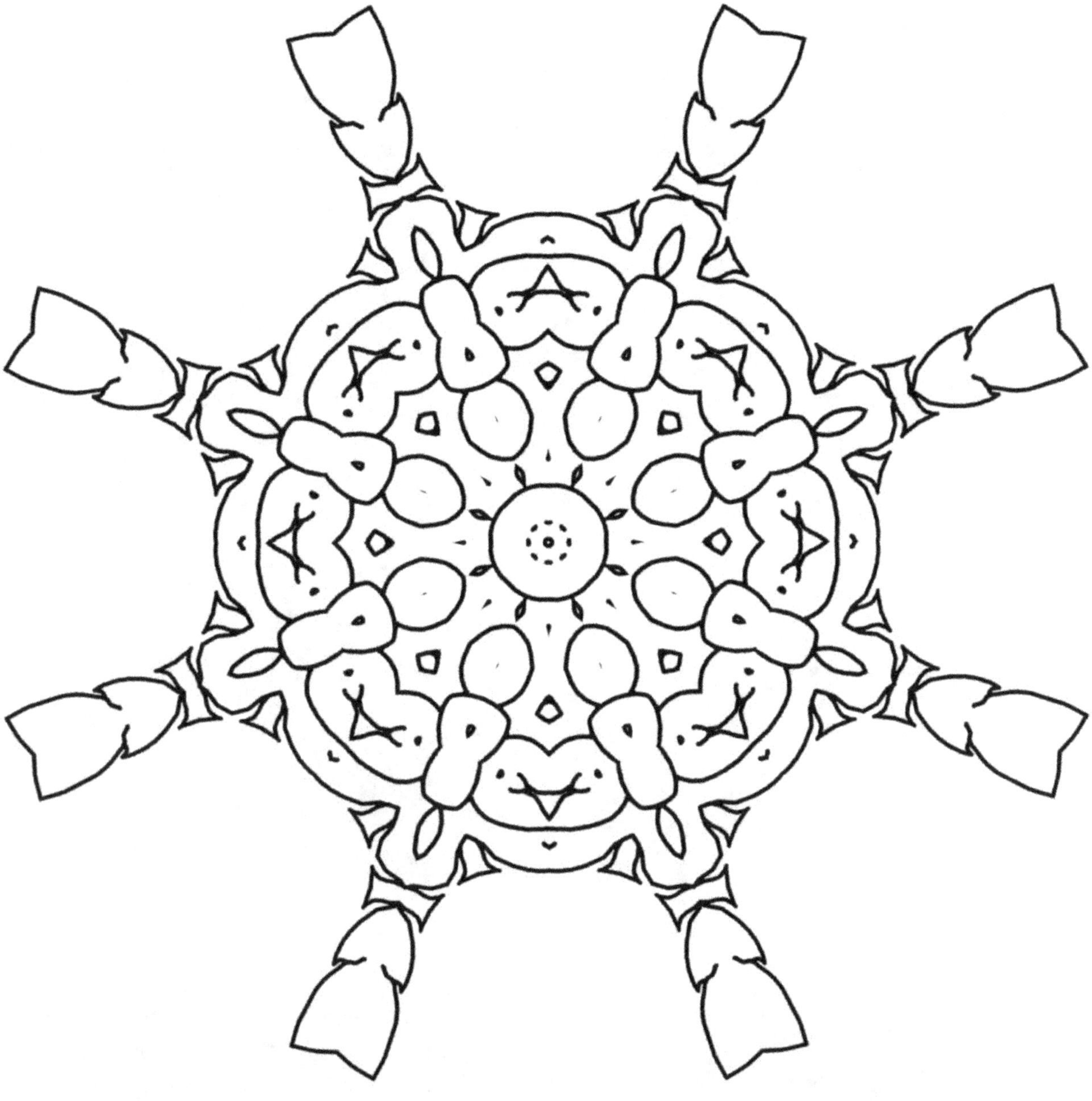

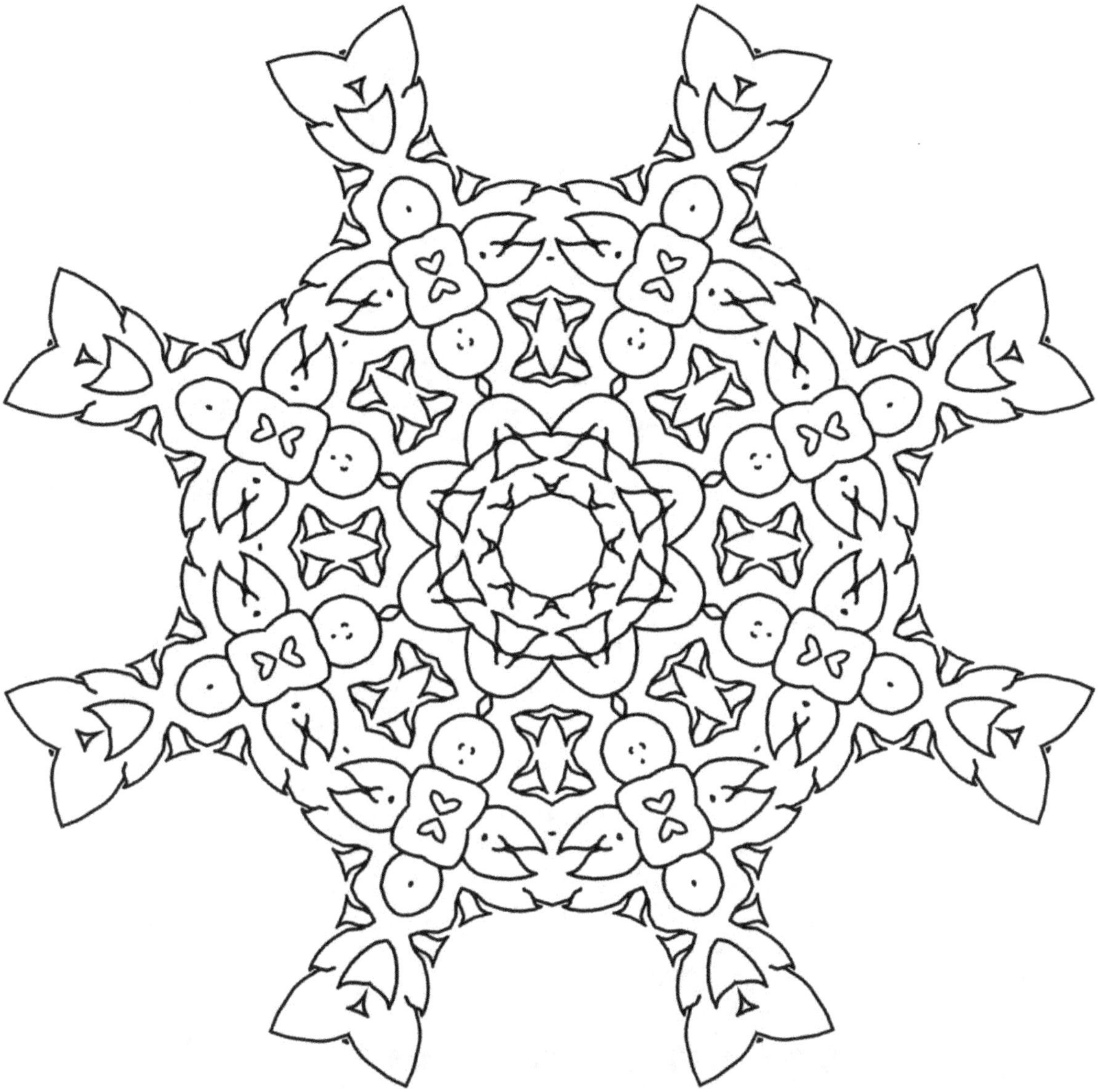

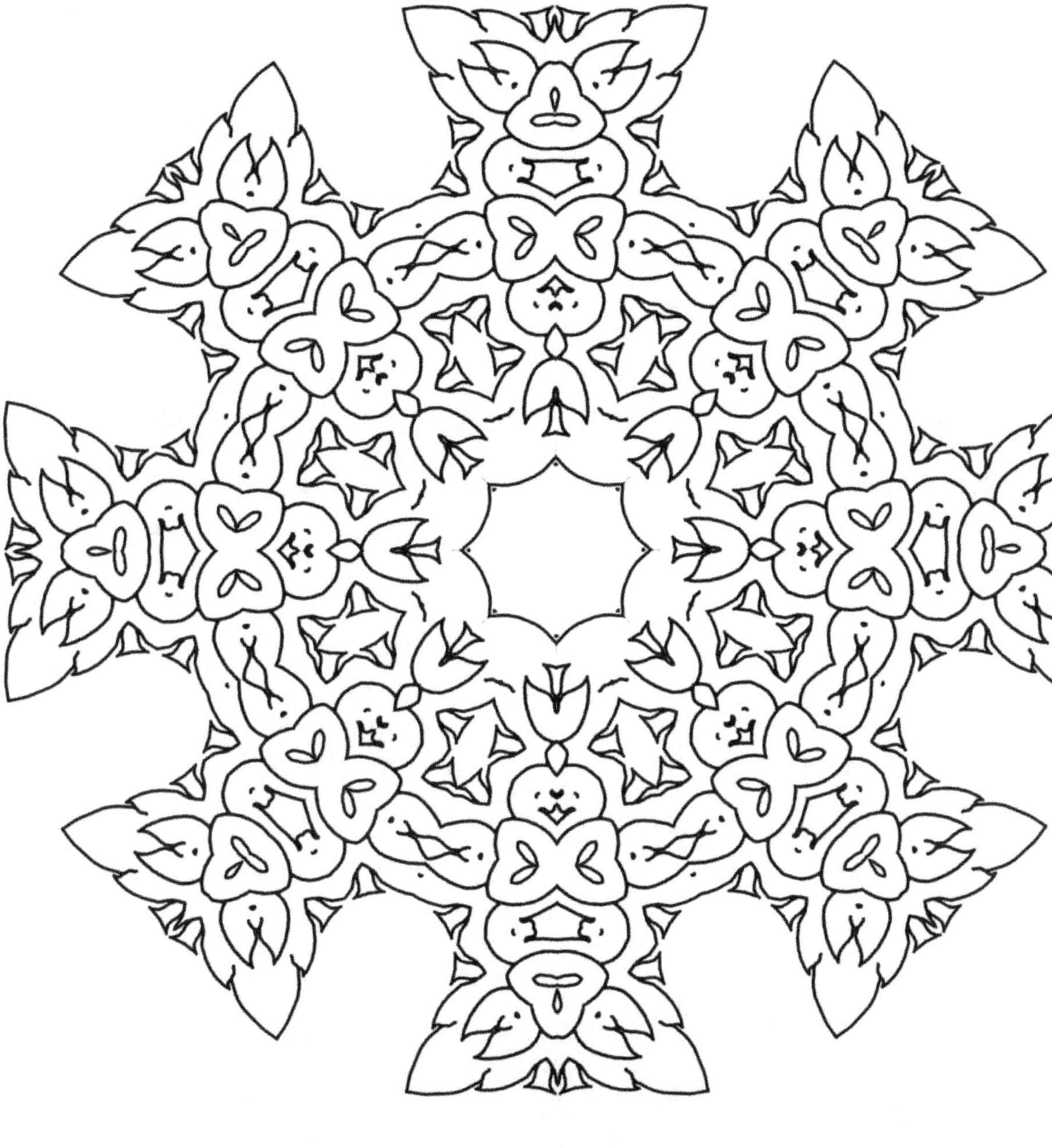

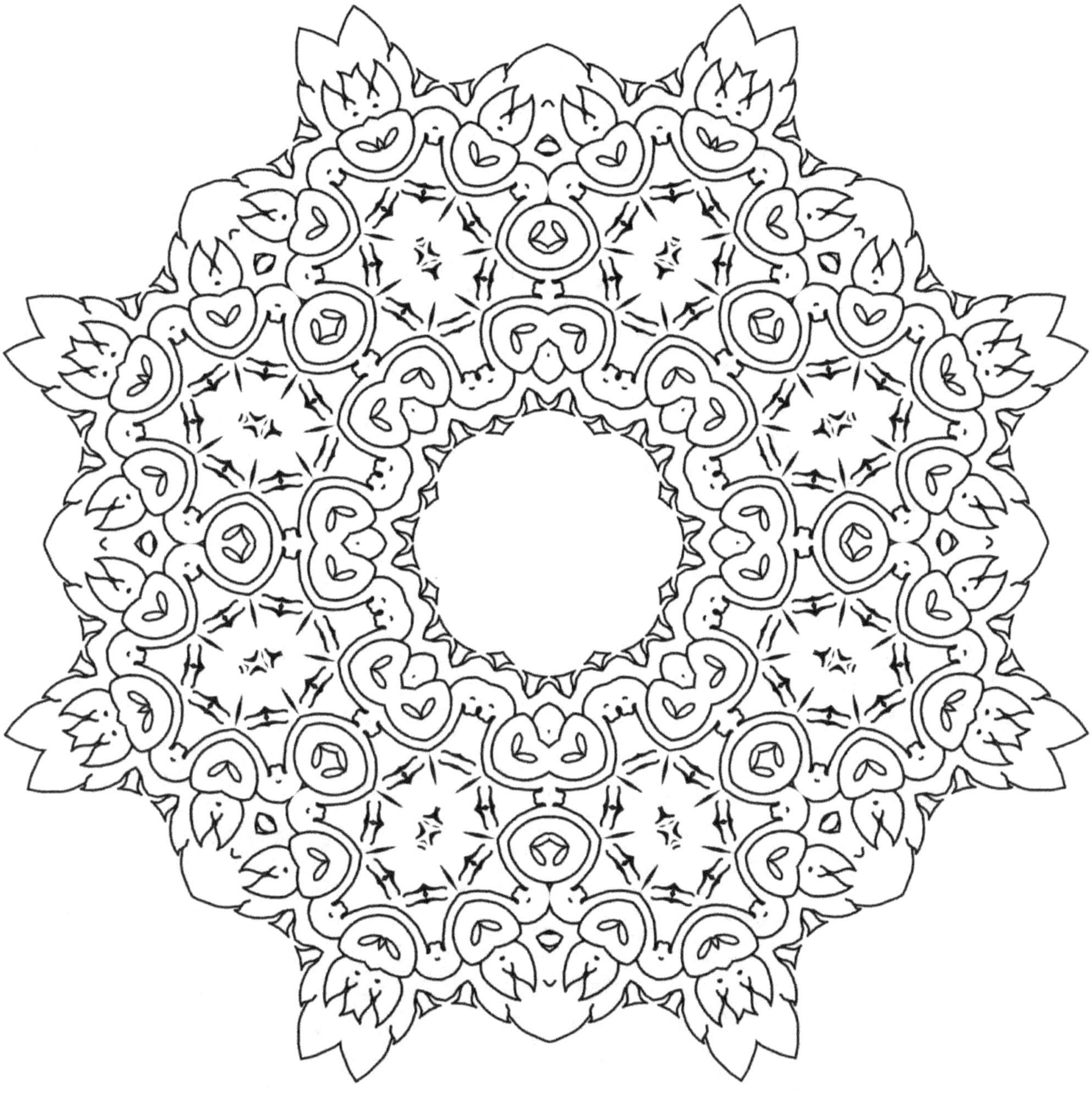

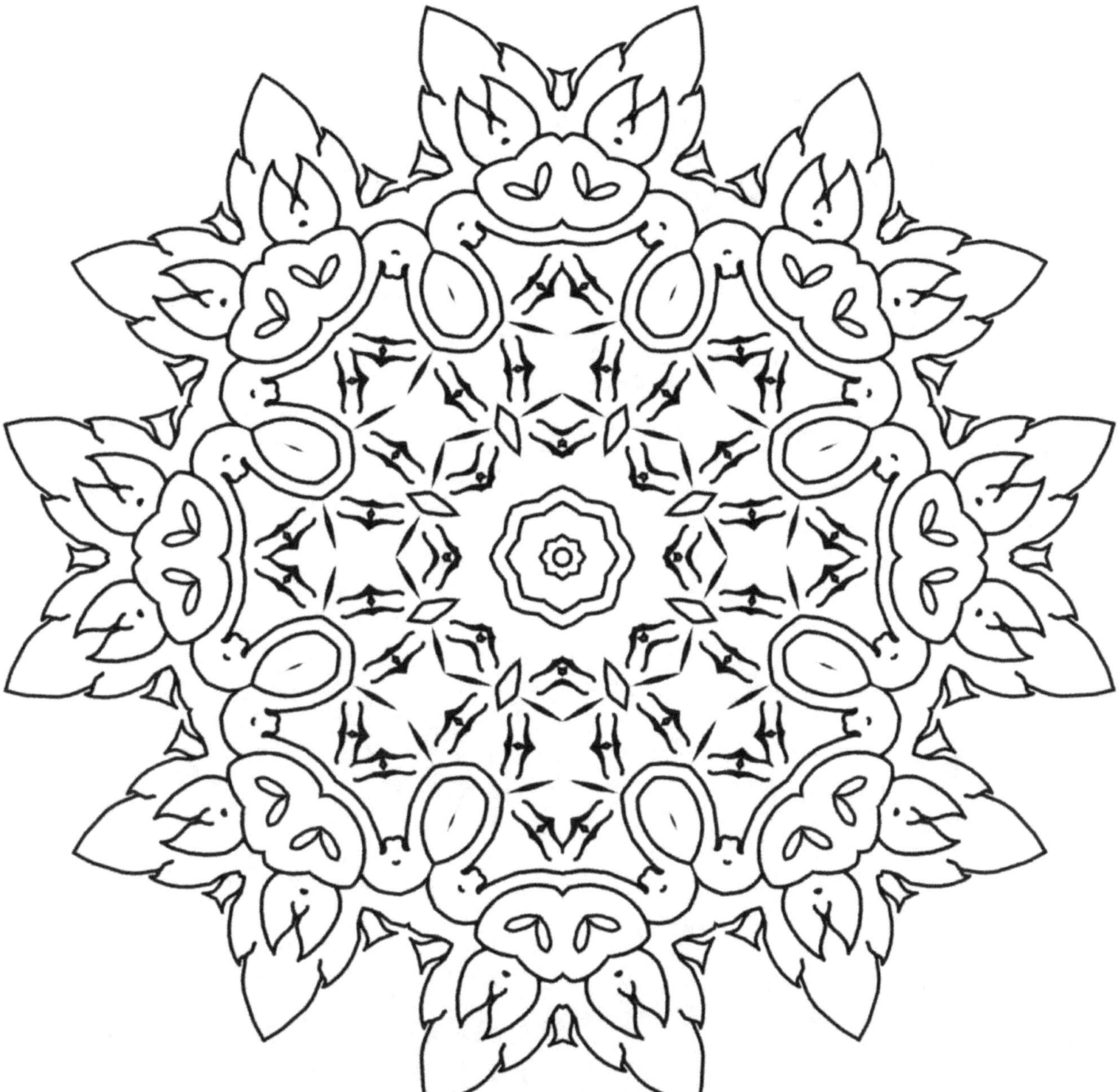

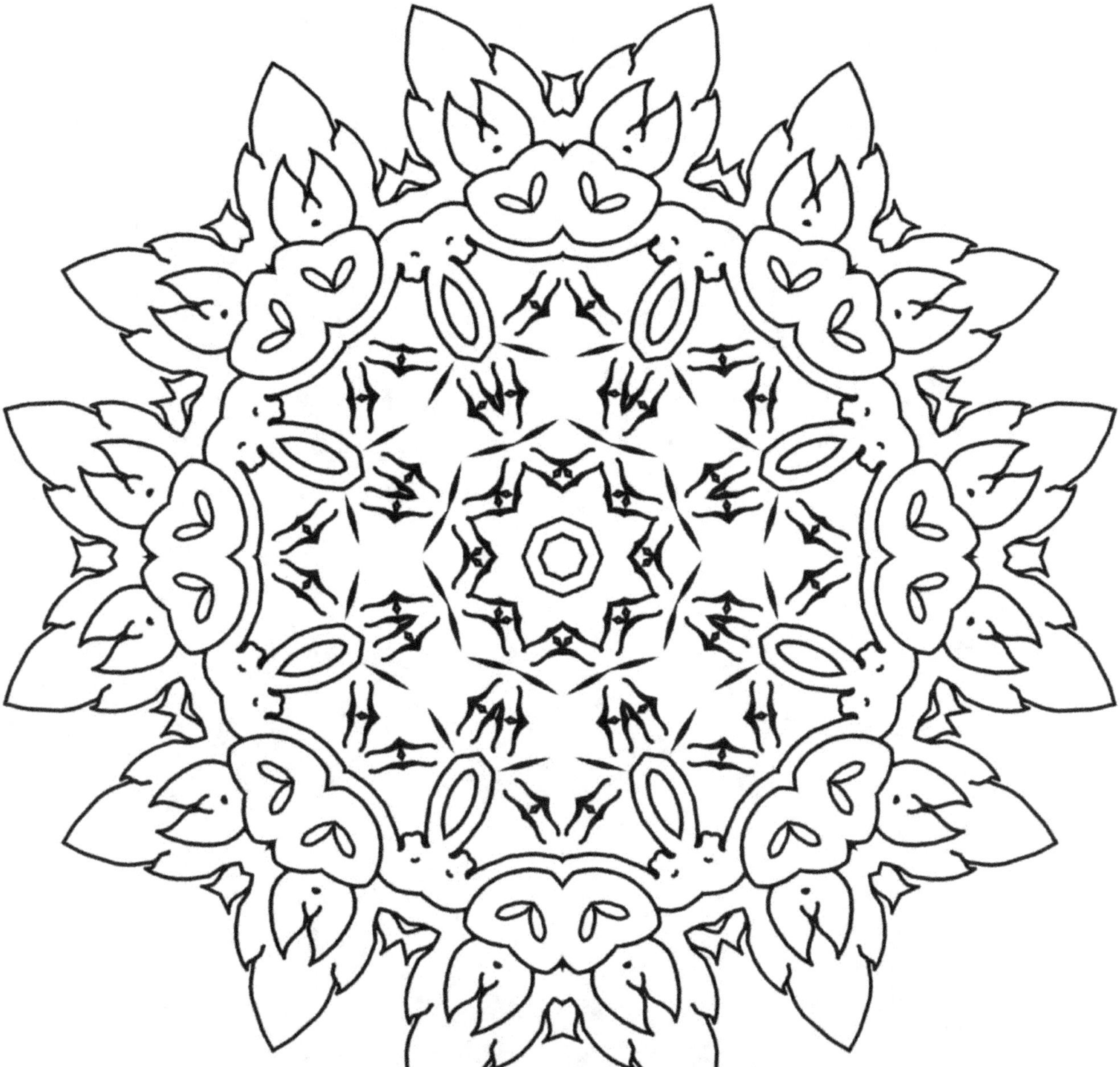

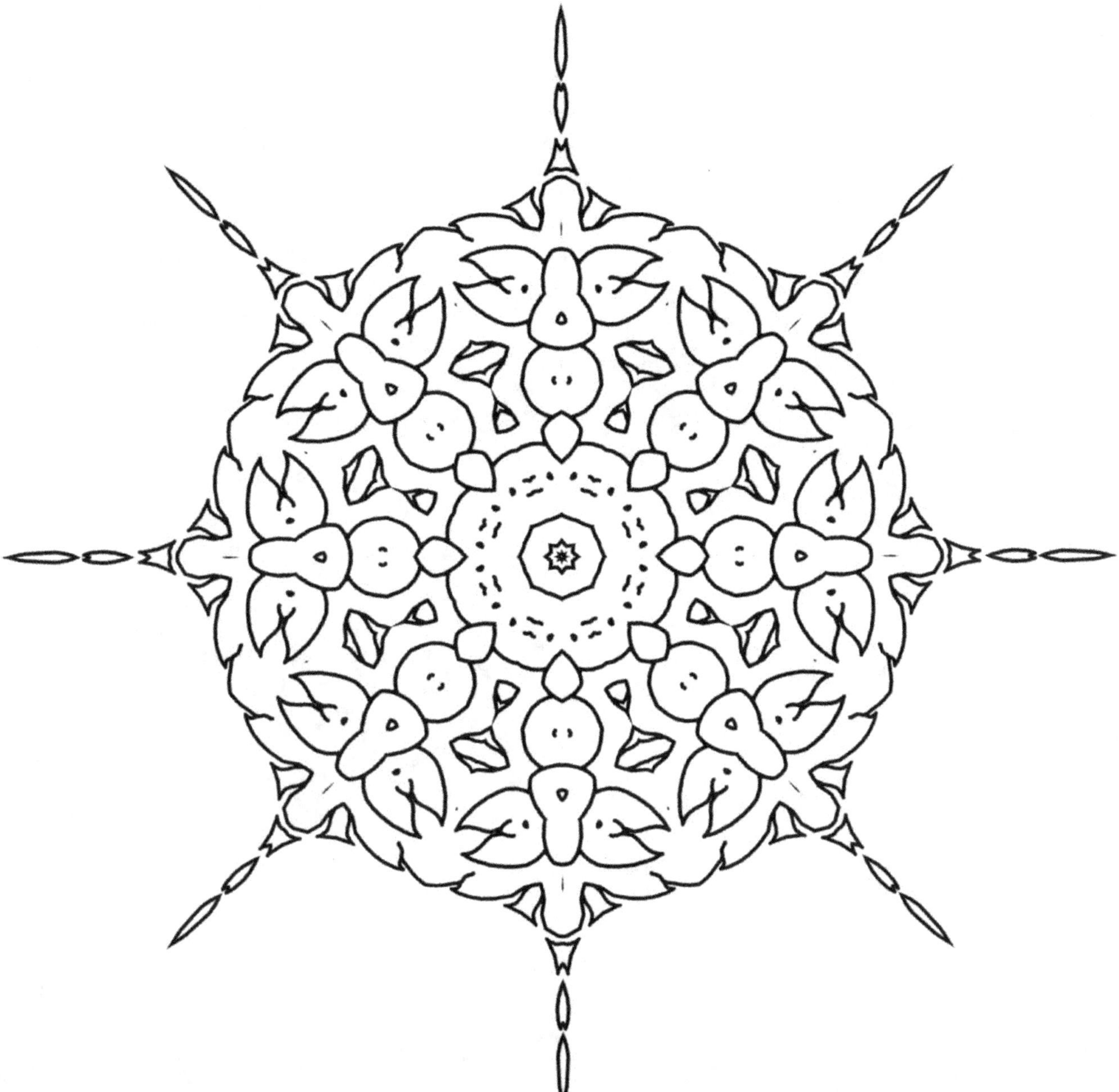

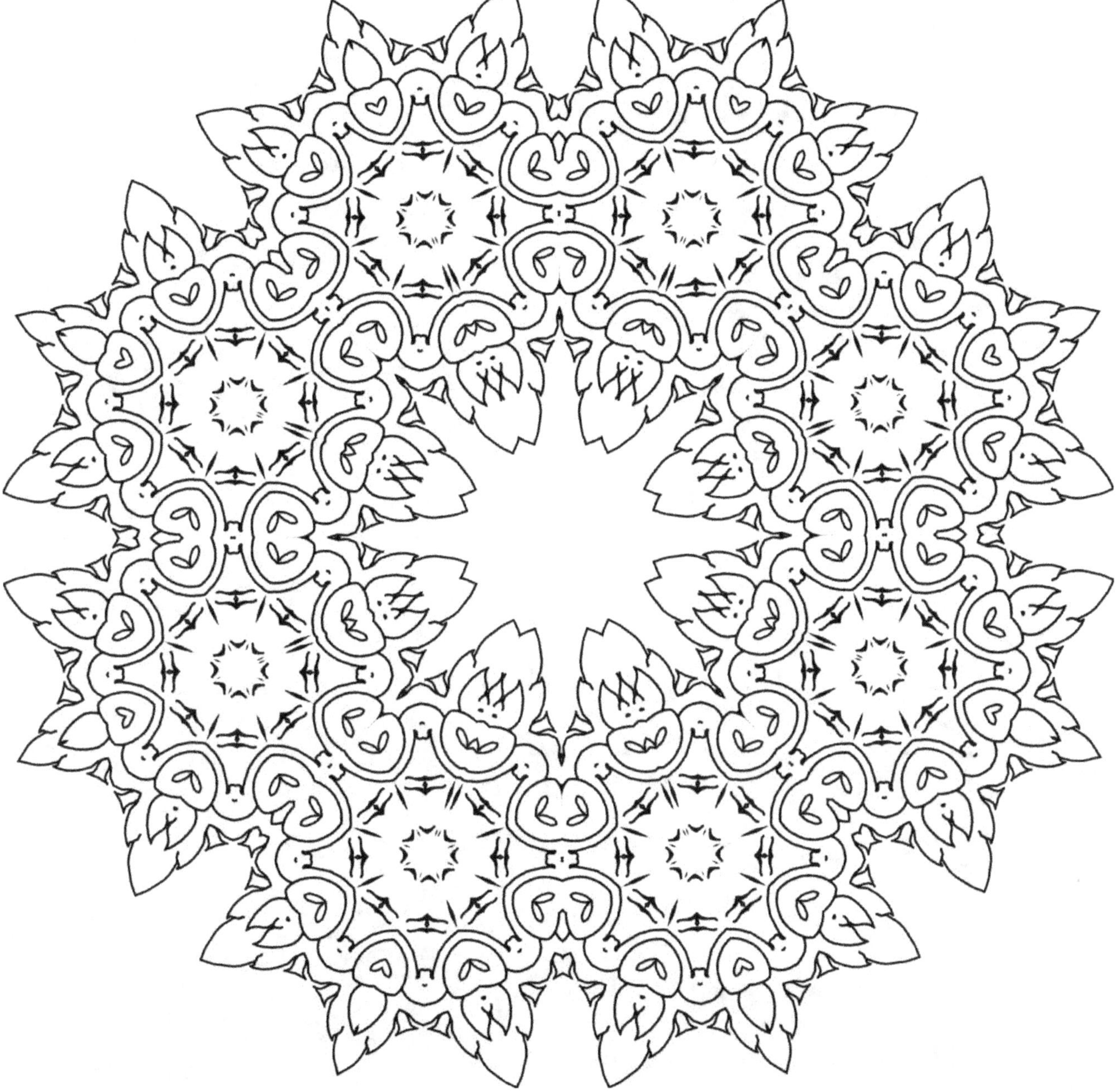

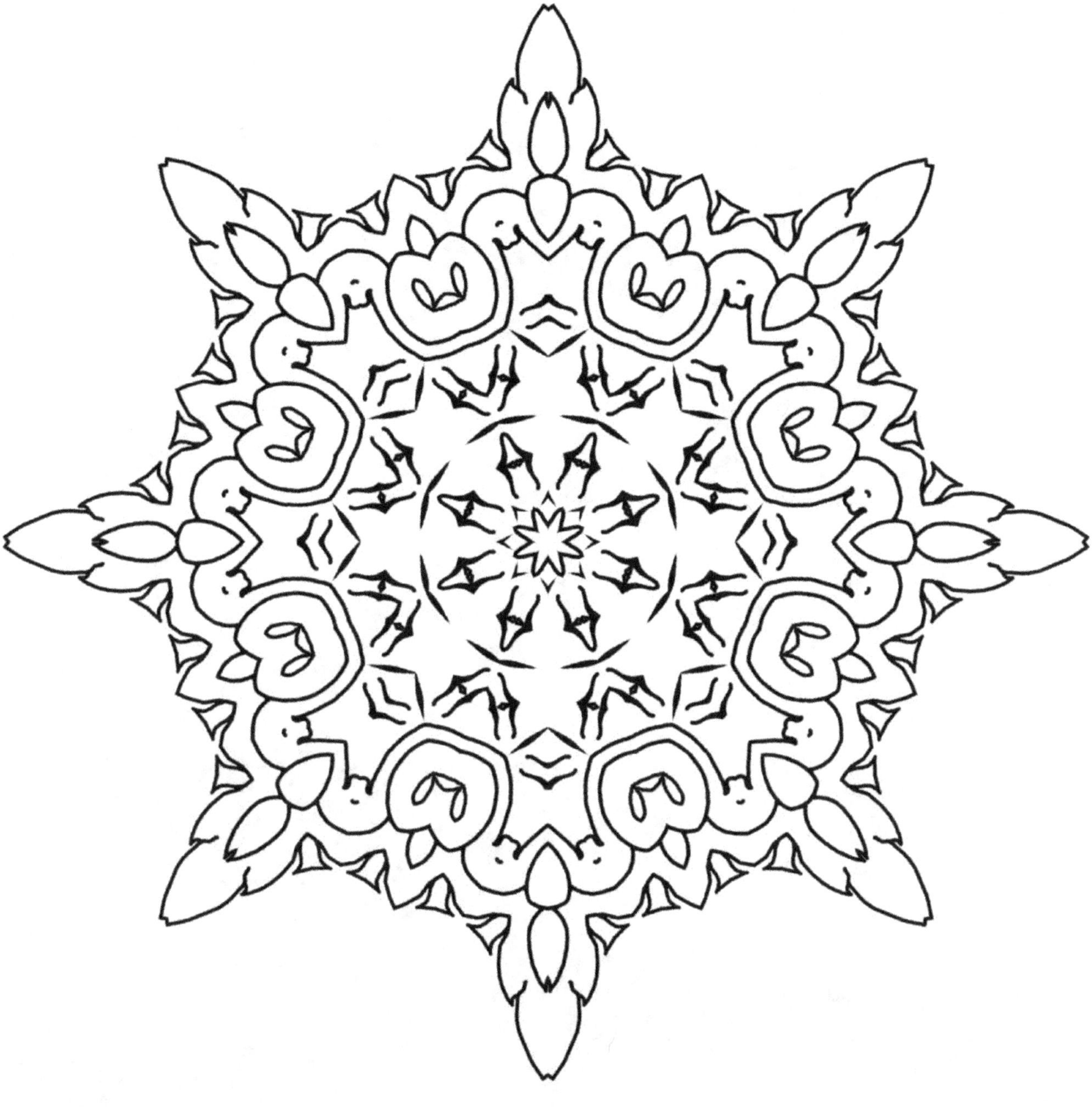

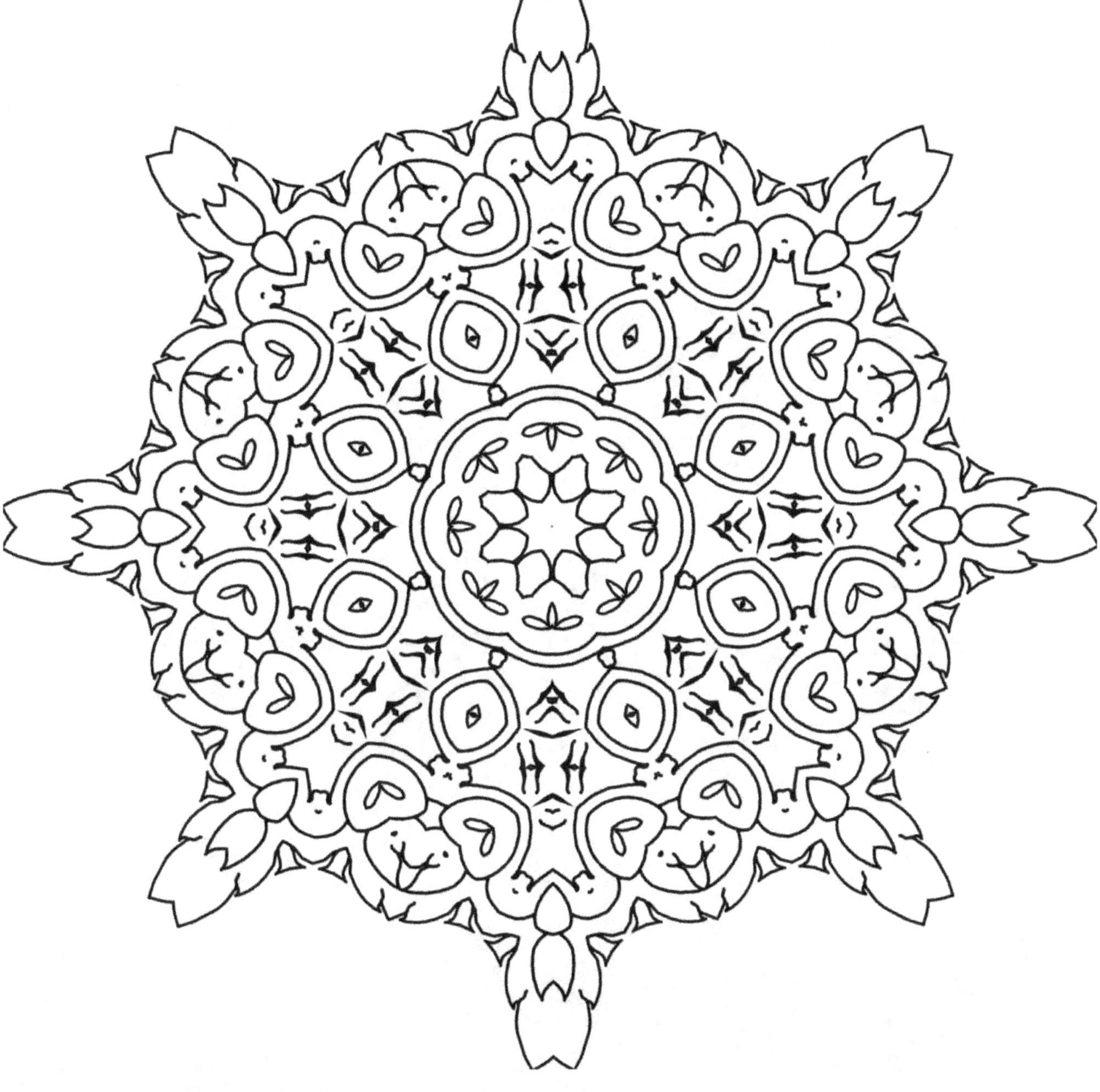

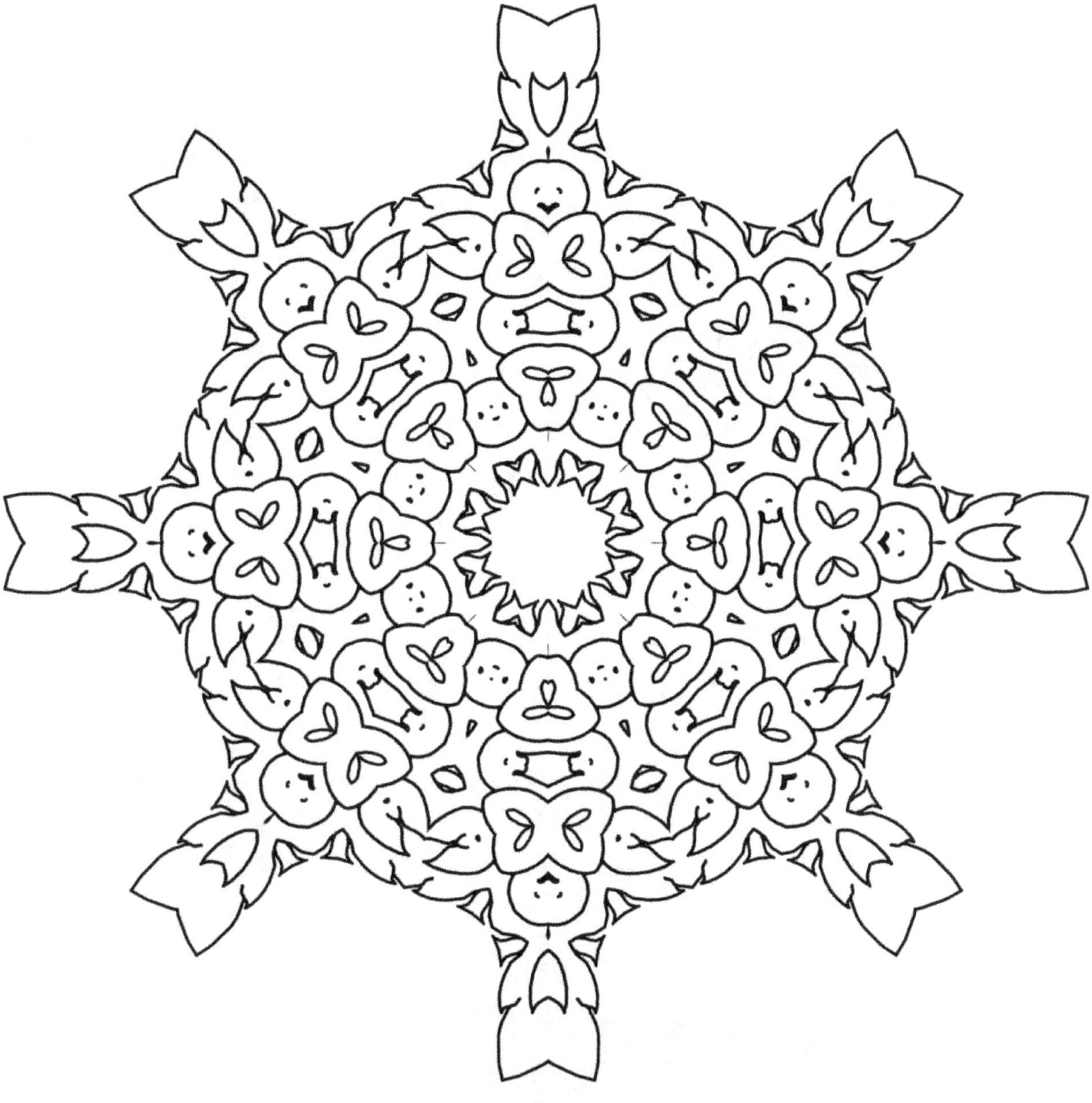

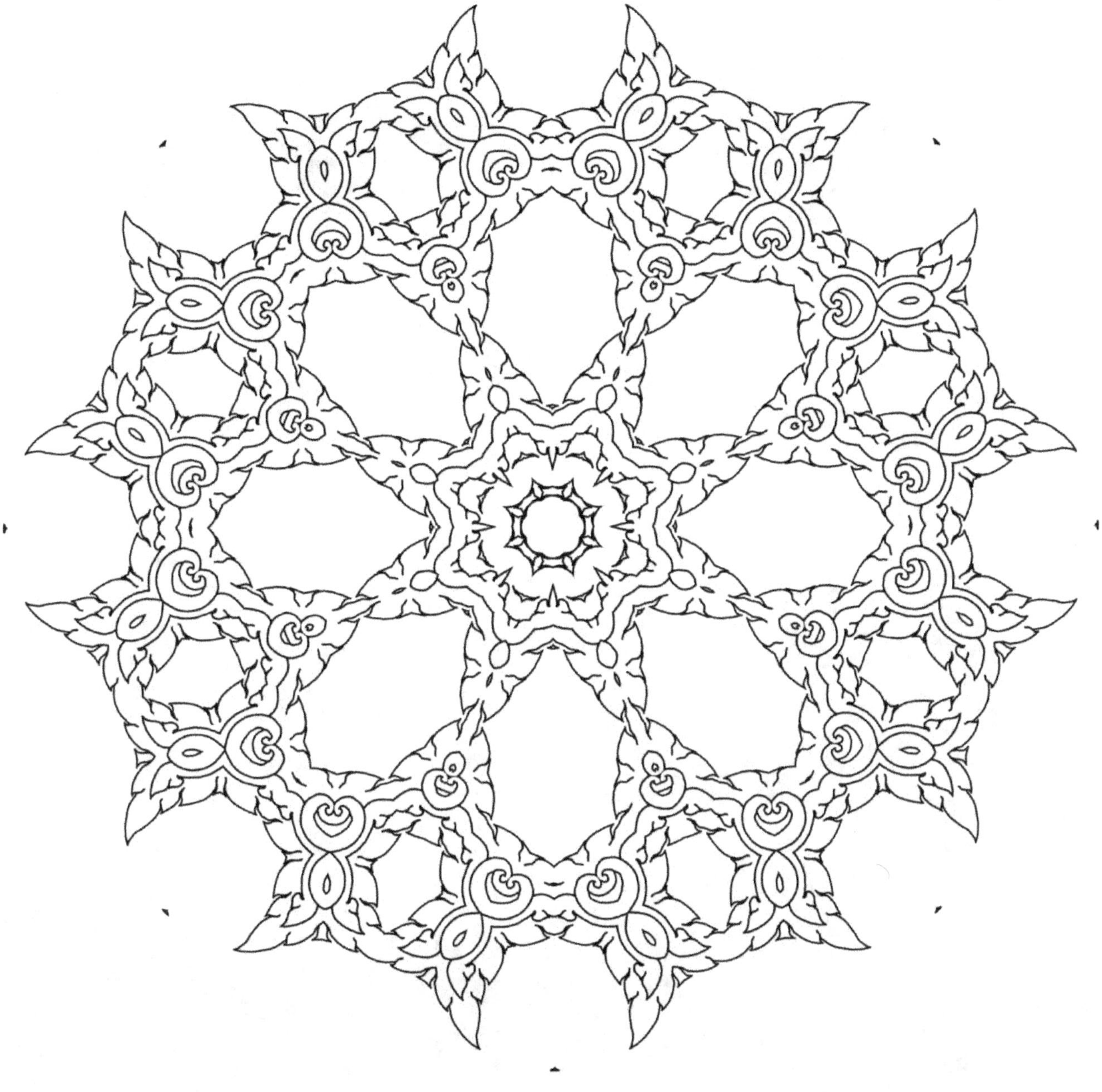

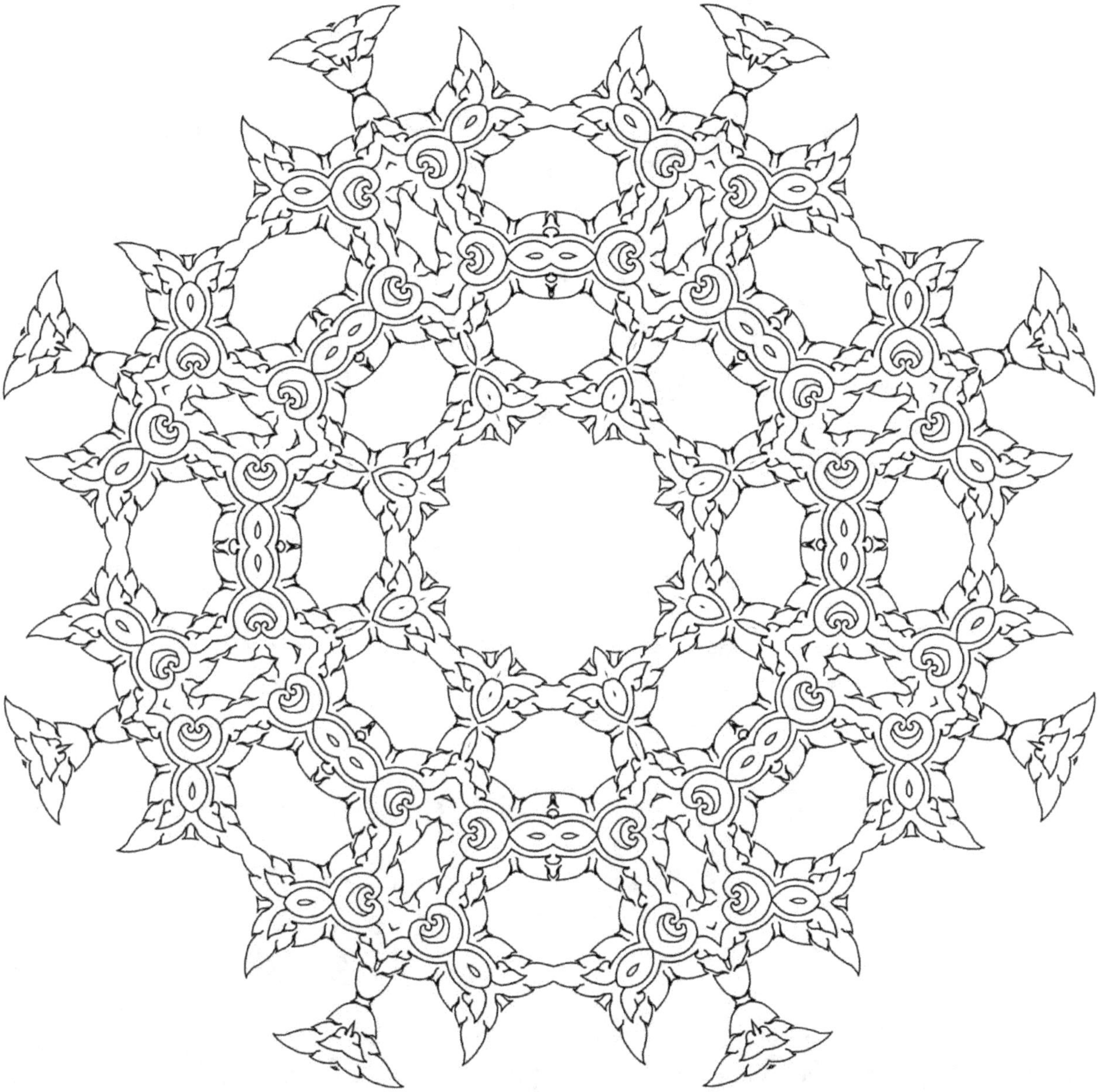

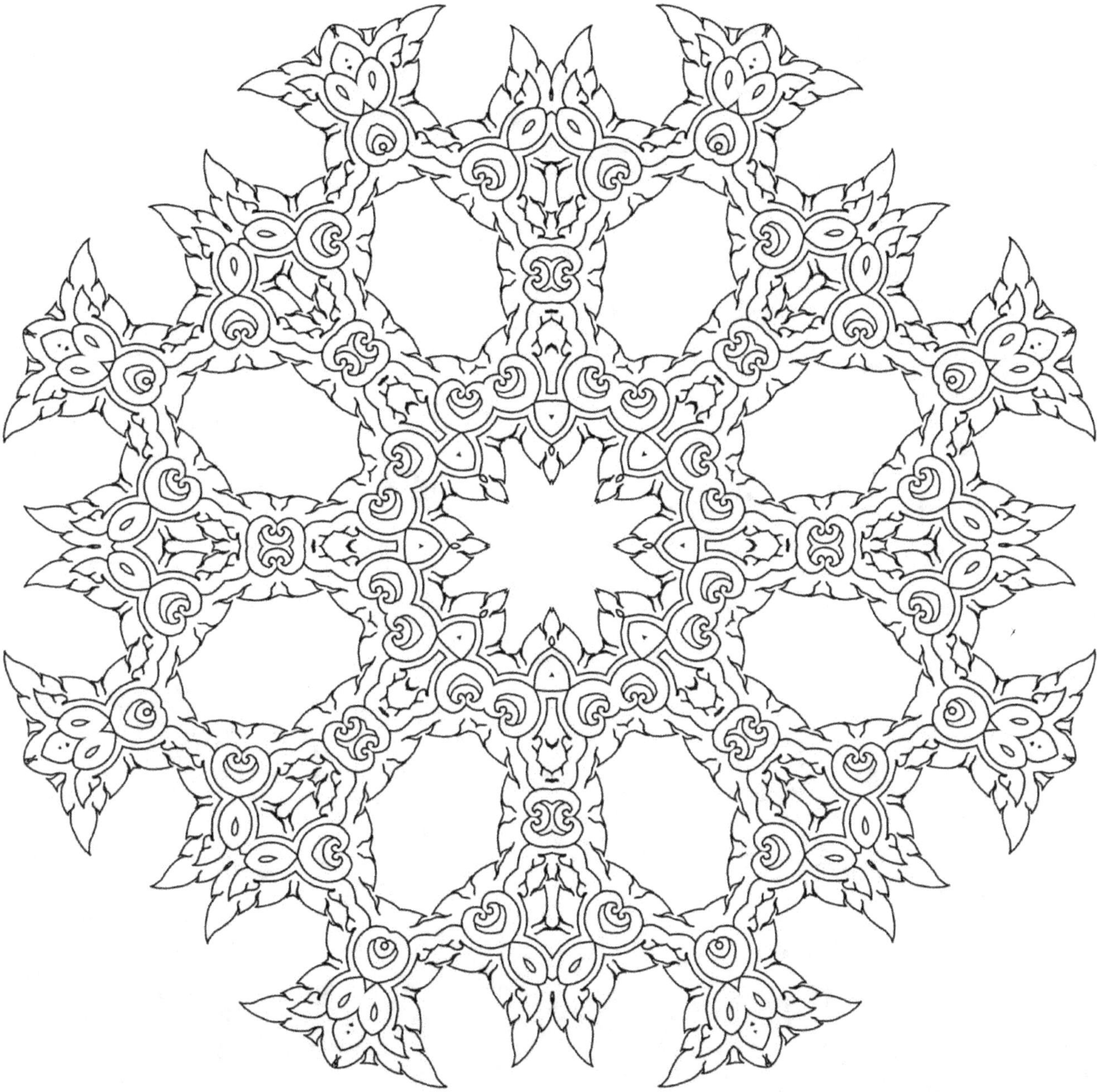

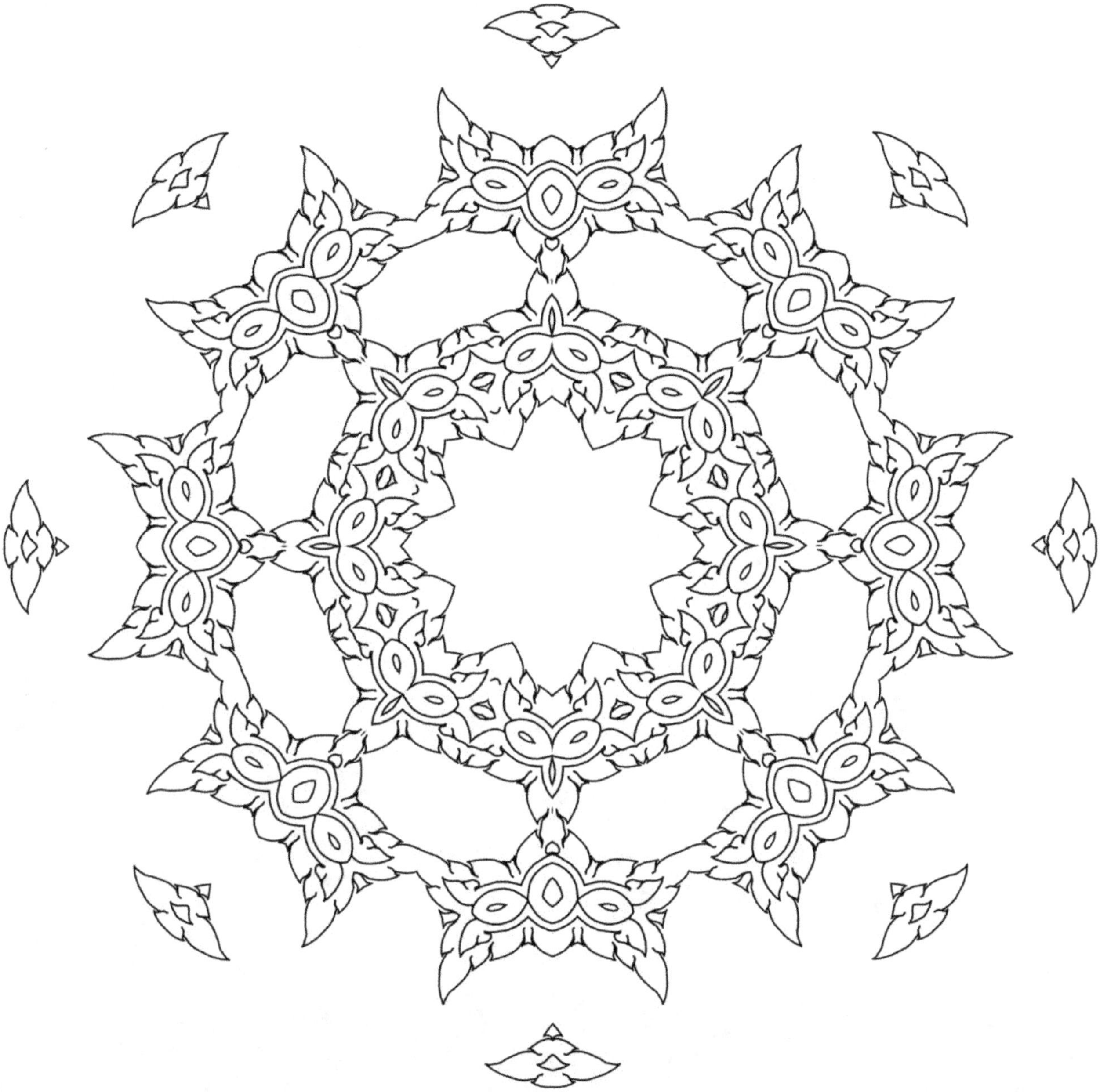

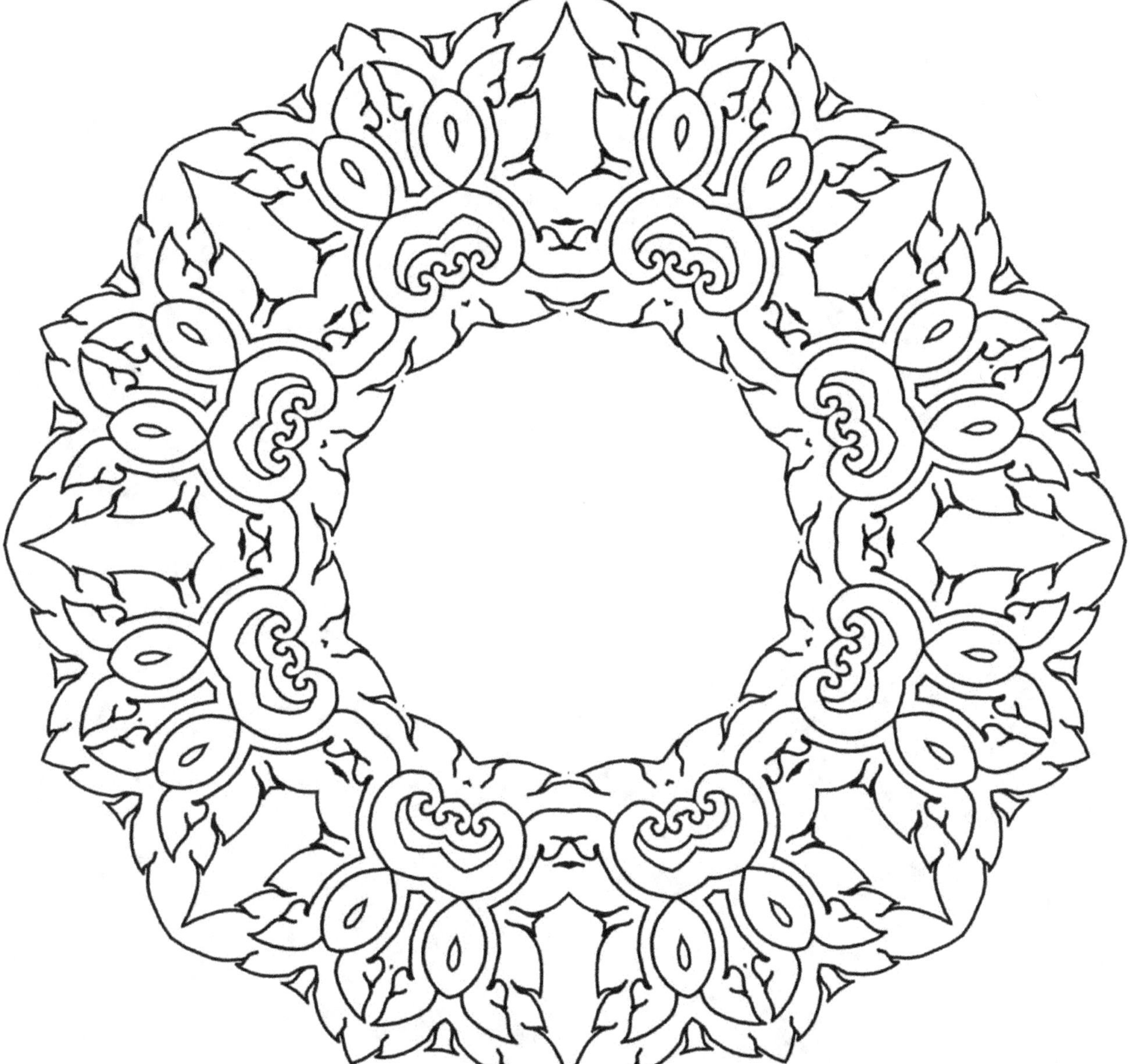

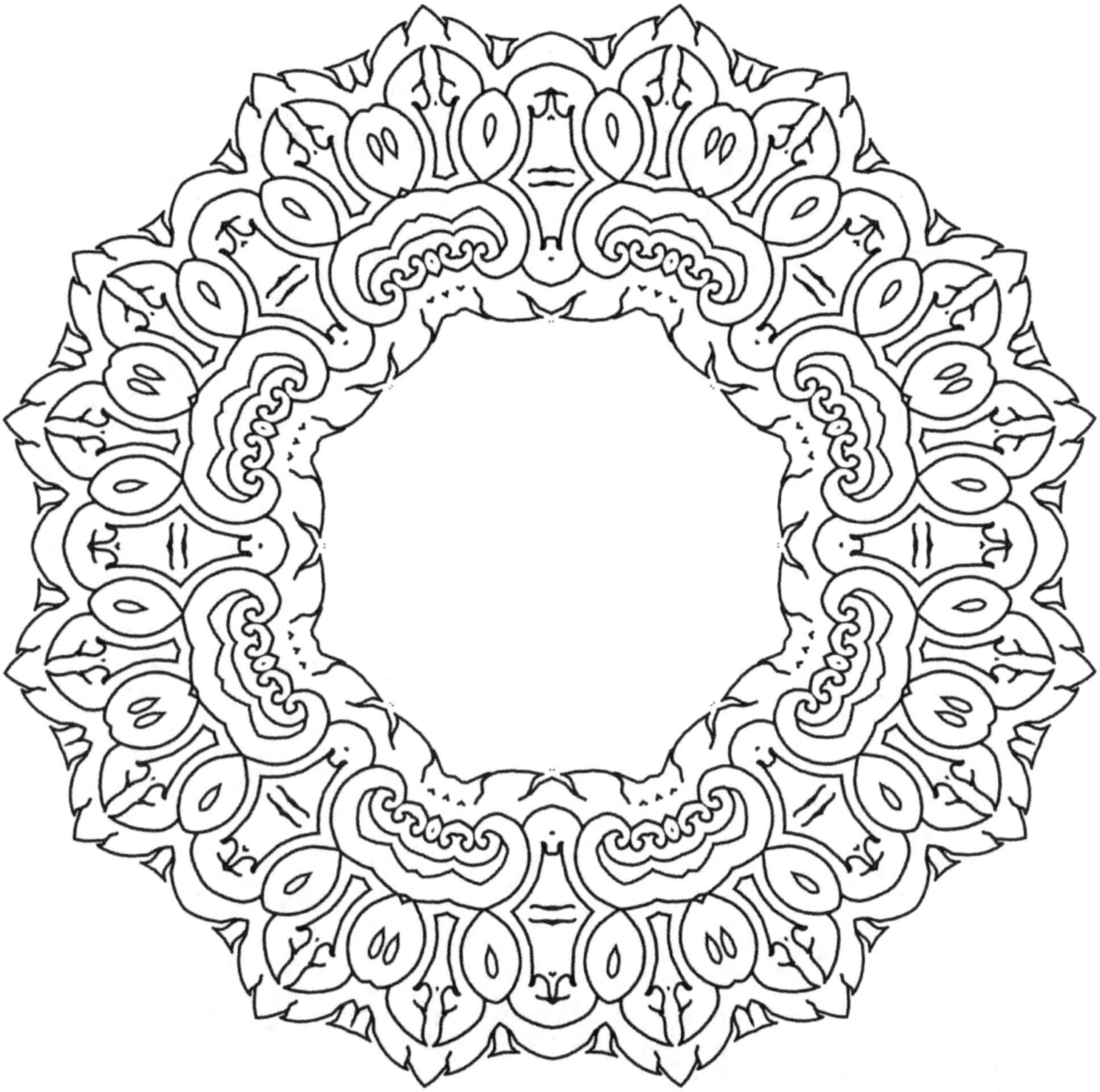

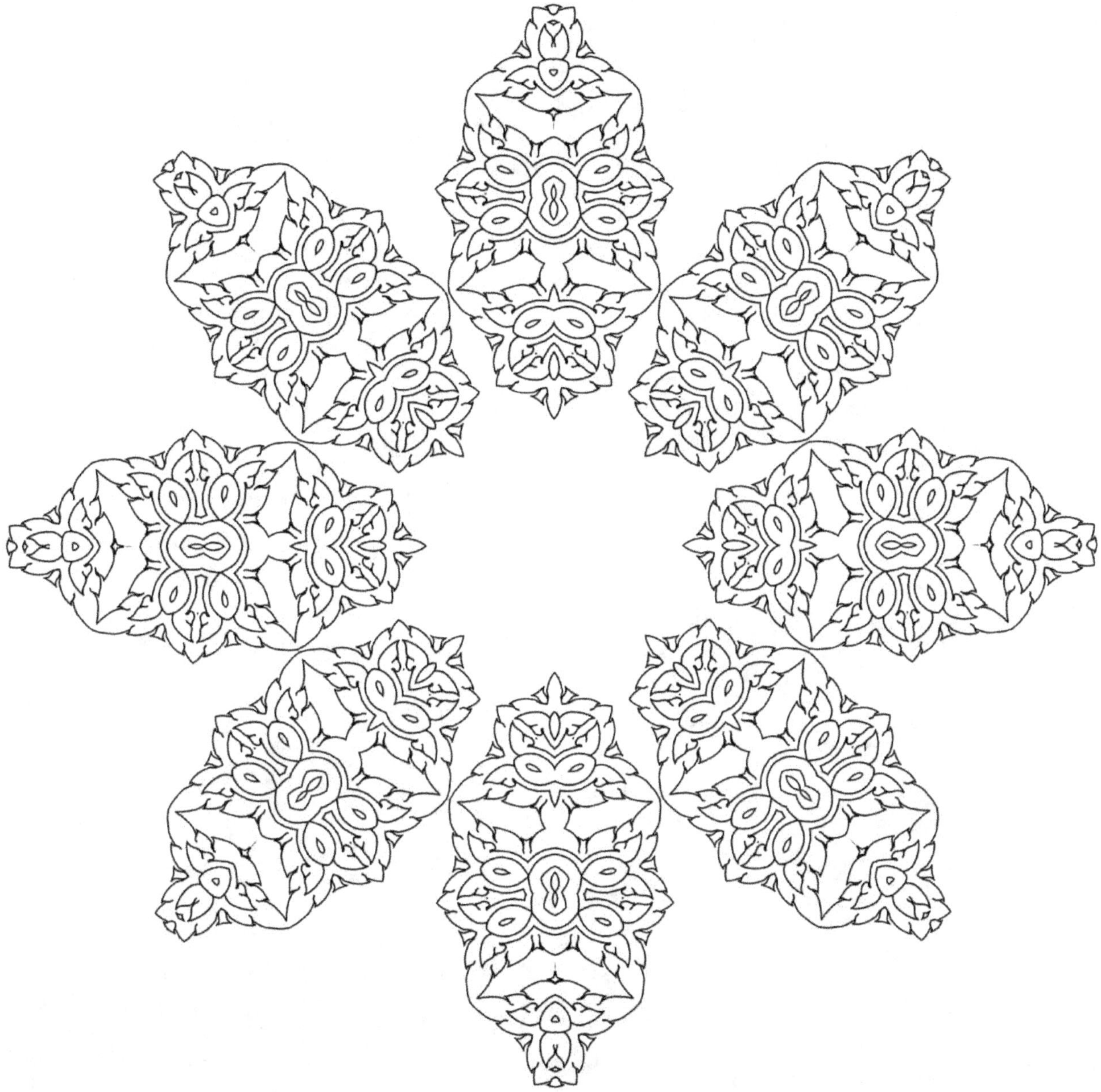

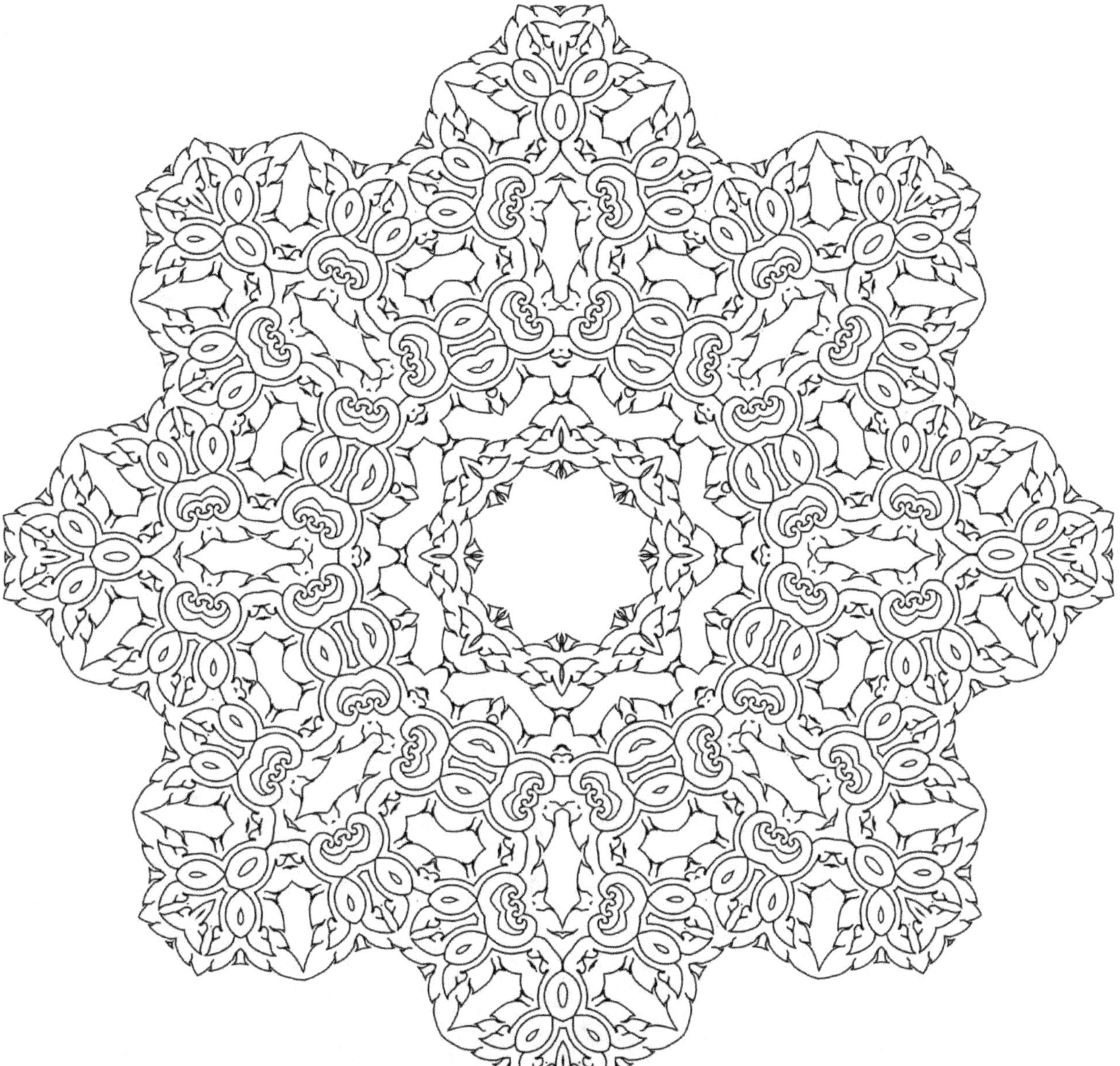

Thank you

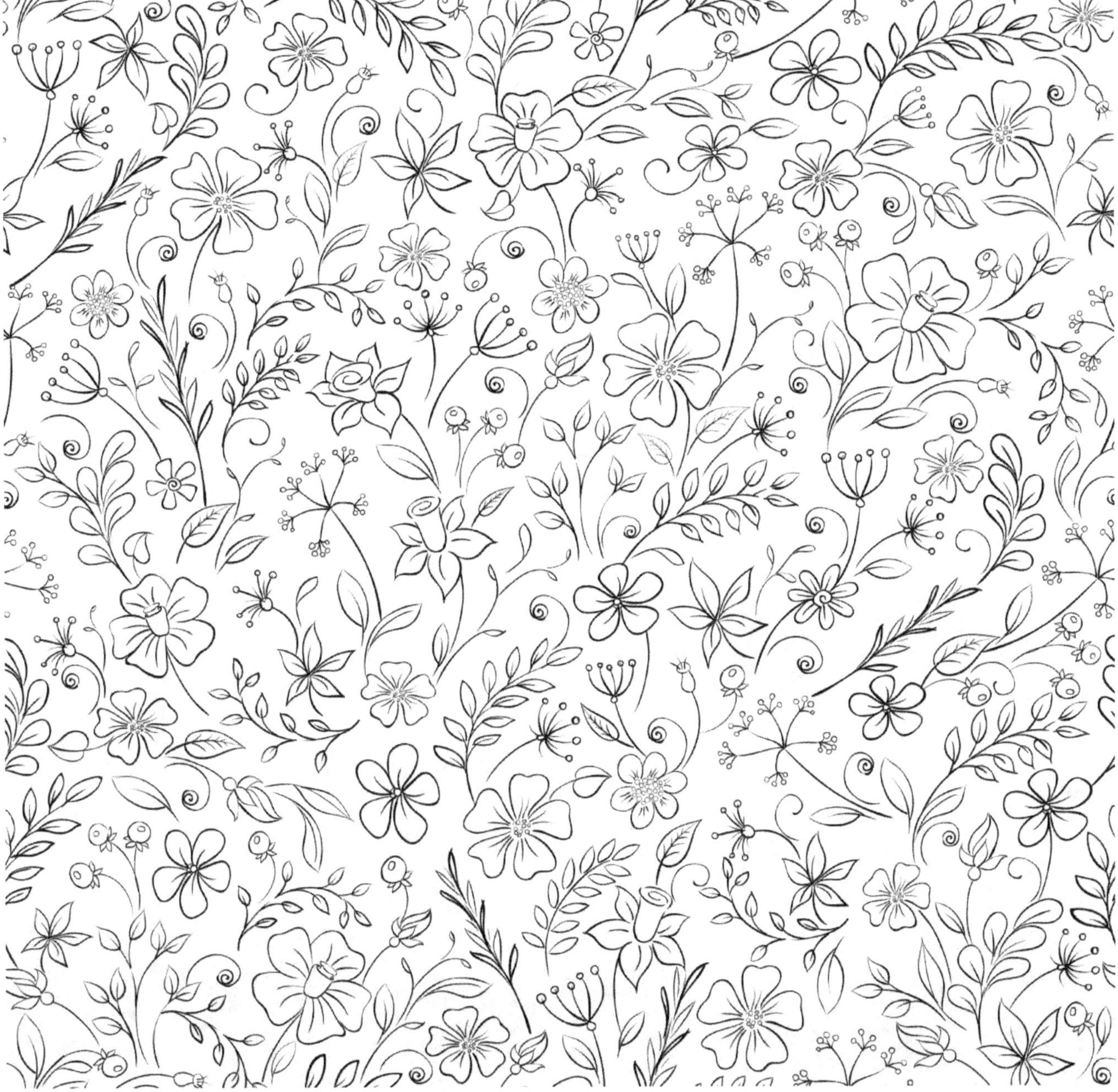

www.ingramcontent.com/pod-product-compliance
Lightning Source LLC
Chambersburg PA
CBHW081116180526
45170CB00008B/2863